Why I

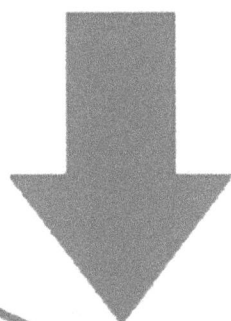

FAILED

in the Creative Arts

Why I

in the **Creative Arts**
and How
NOT to follow
in my Footsteps

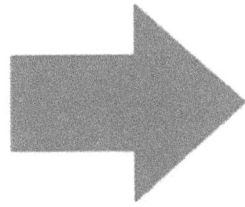

Steve Grossman

WordCrafts

Published by WordCrafts Press
Tullahoma, TN 37388
www.wordcrafts.net

CONTENTS

To my patient, understanding and supportive family: Jill, Kayce and Jennah. I am blessed beyond measure.

INTRODUCTION

FAILED

I was a musician once, and now I'm not.

Well, perhaps it's more correct to say I used to make my living as a musician, and now I don't.

Either way, it means the same thing: I'm not in the arts anymore. For reasons I didn't fully understand at the time, my career path went up, leveled off, and then went down.

The leveling off was the most confusing part.

I knew how to play drums and I was a nice guy, but I constantly saw other people get the gigs I wanted. Despite having the talent to get the gigs, the success I wanted never came, and I didn't understand why.

Until I joined the "Real World."

The Real Problem

"Real World" is a term Creative Artists use to mean anything outside of the "The Arts". They use it in phrases such as, "This sure beats making a living in the real world," or "It didn't work out, so I'm getting a job in the real world."

When people in the Real World tell people in The Arts to "quit dreaming and get a real job," Creative Artists say: "If I do, I'll be a sellout."

These terms imply the "Real" and "Arts" worlds are separated by a big wall; a wall that should not be climbed or looked over because the rules and rewards of each world are different.

I used to think that way. I wish I hadn't.

Creative Artists think they are different. Of course everyone thinks they are unique and special, but people in The Arts go further. Their uniqueness is worn boldly and proudly. The more unique something is - a song, concert, outfit, whatever - the better it must be. It's "Artsy."

There is even some obvious and not so obvious prejudice against people who are not artsy enough. This prejudice divides The Arts from the Real World, and even divides groups of Creative Artists.

I used to think that way. I wish I hadn't.

Creative Artists have a death grip on their dreams. Because they constantly hear, "You'll never make it," and "Go get a real job," they close their minds to any outside influence or ideas.

I used to also think that way. I wish I hadn't.

Lastly, Creative Artists struggle with success. They believe they should only be "in it for the art!"

I used to think that way, too.

Just Out of Reach

I had a pretty good run in the arts. As I look back over my 20 years of playing drums in the industry, I have no complaints. I accomplished a bunch of my goals and achieved more than most creatives ever do.

But my ultimate career goals always seemed just out of reach, and I could never figure out why. I saw and experienced things that left me confused and frustrated; things that gave me questions and doubts that eventually caused me to leave the business.

Leaving music - my one and only passion - was hard. But as I worked to retrain myself so I could provide for my family, I found a world of information about ideas and skills that I never knew existed.

This information gave me answers; answers to why I didn't get gigs and other musicians did; answers to why I got some gigs and others didn't. I learned why I thought the things I thought - and why some were good and some were not; and why I had partly succeeded, but ultimately failed.

The more I learned the more excited I got. For the first time in a long time, I was excited about my future.

But this book isn't about me, it's about you. It's about telling you why

I failed in the creative arts and how not to follow in my footsteps.

So, why did I fail?

- I didn't realize the power of attitudes and beliefs that affected my life for good and bad.
- I didn't know about people skills.
- I didn't know about success skills: things that work for everyone and are never taught in schools.
- I was clueless about money and finances.
- I didn't know what I really wanted.

This Book

I wrote this book as a ladder over the wall between The Arts and the Real World; a ladder that will give you access to the real world skills that will help you succeed with your creative ideas. It will also show you how and why you should always look over that wall for help in building your career.

This book is about:
- **You** - the real you, your art and your dreams; the things that make up your life and therefore deserve your time and attention.
- **Business** - the fact that you are pursuing a career in an industry just like Henry Ford did when he made the first Model T a century ago. Business is business and the more you know about it, the more you'll succeed.
- **Skills** - the tools, skills and ideas that people use to succeed no matter who they are or what they're doing.

What this book is NOT about:
- You will not find me dogging the creative or entertainment industries or any of their people. Are there problems and bad

people in these industries? Of course, just like the real world. But overall, the creative arts are full of great people and can be a fun way to make a living - if you can.

- I will not tell "Arts" people how to understand or deal with "Real World" people or vice-versa. You might learn some of that along the way, but that's not my goal.
- You will not find a list of publishers, managers, agents, advice about contracts, performance techniques, or how to do your hair and make-up. There are tons of books and resources that cover all that stuff and more. Use them all – you need that information to succeed, too.

My purpose is to show you what you need to learn from the Real World, how you can use it to build your career, and why you should.

First, I have a story:

Mike and Bill

Imagine a small duplex in the suburbs of an average city. On one side of the duplex there lives a man named Bill. Bill works as a banker. On the other side there lives a man named Mike. Mike works as a guitar player.

It's 6:15 in the morning when Bill's alarm goes off. Bill gets up bleary eyed and heads for the shower to get ready for work. Next door, Mike is asleep - really asleep. His band finished playing at two in the morning and he's only been in bed since four.

We'll check on him later.

Twenty minutes later, Bill is clean and shaved, and sipping on a cup of coffee while he picks out a tie. He's got an important meeting today at the bank so he picks his red tie, white shirt and blue suit because he has read countless studies that prove this to be a powerful combination.

At 7:30, Bill climbs into his car - which he bought so he could haul clients around - and begins the 45-minute drive to the office. He arrives at his job and begins to do whatever it is that bankers do. At 10:15 he takes a break, which is the same time Mike turns over, fluffs his pillow and goes back to sleep.

At 1:00 in the afternoon Bill has finished lunch and is giving himself one last check in the mirror before heading to his manager's office to discuss the afternoon's bank merger meeting.

Back at the duplex Mike gets out of bed and puts on some torn jeans and his favorite tee shirt. He skips a shower because his band has an important show tonight and his hair looks best a day or two old. He skips shaving, too. He grabs his guitar, climbs into his van - which he bought so he could haul the band's equipment around - and begins the drive to the drummer's house.

After loading the drums in the van they head to the club for a sound check, a quick rehearsal, and a short meeting with their manager to discuss the evening's record deal meeting. The record label's entire A&R department will be there, and they expect an answer after the show.

It's about 7:00 pm when Mike pulls back in his drive for a quick dinner before the show. He meets Bill coming home from the bank:

"How's it goin' Bill?"

"Pretty good, how 'bout you?"

"Great, we've got our big show tonight."

Bill had forgotten that tonight was the big night for Mike and his band. "Oh, that's right. How does the record contract look?"

"I think it could be cool. The company has a great reputation and the connections to get us the attention and fans we need. I think we're gonna go for it. How's the bank merger look?"

"Thanks for asking, Mike. The other company is well respected and they bring a larger customer base to our operation. The more attention we get, the better it is for business."

"Let me know how it works out, and we'll go out and celebrate our good fortunes!"

Bill turns to go inside and says over his shoulder, "Sounds like a plan, Mike. Good luck tonight."

"Thanks, Bill, you too. Good night."

Mike and Bill both go inside and watch the news while they eat dinner. At 7:45 Mike changes into his stage outfit – a pair of torn jeans and a tee shirt – checks his hair, and heads off to pick up his girlfriend on the way to the gig. Bill changes clothes, calls his girlfriend and makes plans for lunch the next day. He sits back and settles in for a night of ESPN.

At 10:00 PM Mike is giving himself one more check in the mirror before hitting the stage. Back at the duplex Bill climbs into bed, shuts off the lights and thinks as he drifts off to sleep: _It's been a long, but productive day._ He's excited about his bank joining forces with the other bank. It's a good move for the bank and for him.
Five hours later - as Bill turns over, fluffs his pillow and goes back to sleep - Mike's band has just finished a smokin' set and had a great

meeting with the label folks. The gear's been packed up, his girlfriend's been dropped off and he thinks about the day as he drives home: *It's been a long, but productive day.* He's excited about his band joining forces with the record label. It's a good move for the band and for him.

ॐ ॐ

Why the Story?

Two different and separate lives in two different and separate worlds, right?

Wrong.

I don't think there are any differences at all. None. Nada. Zilch.

I know what you're thinking: "What about Heavy Metal bands? Surely you don't mean those guys are just like doctors?" Yeah, I do.

"But what about the girls on *So You Think You Can Dance?* You can't mean those girls with their tight pants and halter tops are the same as mechanics?"

Yes, I do.

Now, if you're like most people, you'll tell me that they dress differently, and they act differently, and they do things differently, and they do completely different things. You'll tell me that creatives are *pursuing the dream* while the doctors and mechanics *have jobs.* You'll tell me that the success of an artist depends on talent while doctor or mechanic's success depends on skill. You might even say that creatives are *expressing themselves* while the others just *do work.*

And you might be right; at least on the surface. But if we dig deeper, I think you'll agree with me that artists and doctors and mechanics are not all that different. So, let's start digging.

CHAPTER 1

I THOUGHT TALENT WAS ENOUGH

I auditioned for Barbara Mandrell and she was impressed.

It was sometime in 1989 or '90 and I was hoping to move from the contemporary Christian side of the music business over to country. I wanted to stretch myself and have more chances for work. It wasn't exactly the gig I wanted, but I needed the work and thought it would be good exposure and experience. So, I tried out.

We played through the audition songs and even jammed on a few more. I got lots of nods and compliments and then they discovered I could sing. We stood around the piano and sang through some of Barbara's hits.

I got more nods and compliments, and Barbara was especially glad because not only could I sing, I could sing high. She even joked that she was jealous because I could sing higher than her.

They hired a guy who had a drum suit.

They hired a guy who, in addition to playing great drums, had put little pickups all over a set of coveralls - coveralls that were wired to a drum machine run through the speakers. He could put on the suit, dance around the stage and still play the drums.

Clever guy.

I failed in the creative arts because I thought talent was enough.

The Many Things Needed For Success

In the first paragraph of the story of Mike and Bill we were introduced to two guys living in a city. This means:

- They're making a living and,
- A living can be made anywhere.

I want you to know that you can make a living in the arts and live anywhere you want.

All it takes is money.

The Importance of Making A Living

People in "The Arts" and people in the "Real World" share a common bond: they get hungry and they need shelter, so they go to work. They go to work to make money, so they can buy food and pay for shelter.

> "Money is not the most important thing in life, but money does affect everything that is important."
>
> ~ Kim Kiyosaki

I know money is a tricky and sometimes dangerous topic, but it has to be talked about. It has to be talked about because, to paraphrase Kim Kiyosaki, money affects everything.

If you don't agree, than ask yourself this: how long could you live without money?

How would you live?

Would you run out and hunt your dinner, or would you eat a few berries off a bush? When you got thirsty, would you drink some of the nice, clean water out of your local river?

Me? I'd be dead in three days.

People in "The Arts" and people in the "Real World" share a common bond: they need money to survive. Thankfully, it is possible to earn money in the arts. I'll help you find the right work so you can, too.

Questions:
1. When I mentioned money, was your reaction positive or negative?
2. Is it hard for you to imagine earning a living in the arts?
   a. A good living?
   b. A great living?

Your Work Isn't Your Life

Next we read that "Bill works as a banker" and "Mike works as a guitar player." Note that it does NOT say Bill is a banker and Mike is a guitar player.

Why does that matter?

Because you are not what you do, and what you do doesn't make you who you are.

This is a hard idea for creative artists to wrap their heads around. They have spent their whole lives creating art and see themselves as artists. I can relate. I grew up behind a set of drums and thought that what I did was who I was. I didn't just play drums, _I was a drummer._

But we are more than what we do.

Questions:
1. Do you think you are what you do?
2. Can you imagine not playing music?
3. What would that do to your perception of who you are?

4.   Why do you think it matters?

The next section of the story reveals that Bill and Mike both get sleepy, which just proves that work is tiring.

Dressing For The Job

The following morning: "Bill is clean and shaved and sipping on some coffee while picking out a tie. He's got an important meeting today and picks his red tie with his white shirt and blue suit because he knows that countless studies prove this is a powerful combination."

Before I got my first gig in Nashville with Russ Taff (more on that later), I played with a rock band in Dallas and I had the wardrobe to prove it:

- Boots – a scrunch-down suede with a nice heel
- Correctly faded jeans
- Colorful shirts
- Several colorful bandanas (yes, it was the late 80's)
- And long, permed hair that flew all over the place when I played.

I was cool.

After a few years I left that band and landed the gig with The Sweethearts of the Rodeo. I had lived in Texas and had some western clothes, but I had to buy more for the gig - like a cowboy hat that I sometimes accidentally hit with my drumsticks.

Not cool.

Next, I joined the Gibson/Miller Band. We were signed to Sony/Epic, so we had wardrobe consultants who bought us stuff we thought we'd look good in. On the flip side, we had wardrobe consultants who bought us stuff THEY thought we'd look good in.

Guess what happened when I moved to the "Real World?" I bought a new wardrobe. Does anybody see a pattern developing here?

If you're like every other artist I've ever met, you think that everybody in the "Real World" dresses to conform and that you're lucky to be free to express yourself. You're thankful you can wear what you want and not care what anybody else thinks, instead of having a job where you're told what to wear everyday.

You also think that if I filled a room with bankers, you'd know they were bankers in less than two seconds. Doctors, too – wouldn't the white lab coats be a dead giveaway? Same thing with airline pilots, police officers, and every other profession.

Imagine what would happen if all those doctors, pilots and professionals in the room were dressed like Christian Marclay (visual arts), Johnny Depp (acting), Mario Testino (photography), Rihanna (singer) or Rino Nakasone (dancing)? Wouldn't you say, "Hey, look at all those artists?"

But you'd be wrong. You see, clothes don't *define* what people do; clothes are defined by *what* people do.

People dress to conform to the rules – both spoken and unspoken – of our respective career choices. When a businesswoman dresses for a day at the office she chooses her clothes for exactly the same reasons Beyonce chooses hers.

What are these reasons? Well, some jobs, like a police officer or UPS driver, actually dictate the clothing they wear. But there are other reasons for choosing attire that is appropriate for your career.

First, we all like to be a part of a group of people. If it's a tight knit group that is bound together through some sort of uniqueness it's all the better. Creatives certainly have this bond, but so do autoworkers or computer geeks.

Second, survival. Remember my comment about money and living? Well, I don't think some of the mega-selling singers like wearing some of their get-ups anymore than nurses like their puke-colored smocks, but getting paid a million a year can make any outfit comfortable for a few hours a night.

Take a look around at the next big function you attend and you'll see my point first-hand. If any one of those people were standing in line at the grocery store dressed like that, they would stand out, but put them all together in one room and their outfits are barely noticed. Now, put a successful middle-aged guy in a suit in the room and everybody looks at him weird.

Unless he has money to invest in new talent, then he's the hit of the party!

Questions:
1. Do you own clothes specifically for performing?
2. Clothes for NOT performing?
3. Do you just wear what you wear regardless?

Equipment And Tools

Each of the guys has a vehicle. The banker bought his "so he could haul clients around." Mike bought a van "so he could haul the band's equipment around."

The point is, you're not alone in your need to have the right equipment and necessary tools to do your job correctly. Every occupation has specific tools of the trade, so just keep that in mind when you're complaining about the cost of something you have to have.

Questions:

1. Do you have all the tools and equipment you need for your career? I'll answer this one for you from experience: No. There will always be something cool you want or need.
2. Do you have a plan to get the things you want and need?

Business Is Business

The next section revealed that both Bill and Mike have important meetings to attend.

Bill's bank is considering a merger and Mike's band is discussing "the details of the record contract they've been offered." We've already discussed money and making a living, but this part of the story brings us back to an underlying philosophy about your career that I mentioned in the introduction:

You are pursuing a career in an industry that is every bit as much of a business as the automobile industry that Henry Ford started more than a century ago.

If you get nothing else from this book, please understand that the more you grasp this fact and understand its ramifications the more success you'll find. Yes, it's true that creativity is an art form and it is all about expression. But, it is also a business and THIS IS NOT A BAD THING!

When money is a part of the equation, market forces and business realities must be factored in if you are ever to reach your goals and dreams. Business is not a complicated subject, but it is complex. It's simple if you remember the word, "exchange." What's complex is the number of pieces involved in even the simplest of exchange transactions.

Questions:
1. Why do you think I've stressed the importance of grasping the fact that you are pursuing a career in an industry?
2. Do you think of business as simple or complex?
3. Do you see yourself as a business person?
4. Why?
5. Does defining it as an exchange help or hurt?
6. Why?

People

Bill worked in a bank and Mike played in a band. How could Bill earn money working alone in a bank with the doors locked? Likewise, would it be possible for Mike to make his rent payments sitting in his living room playing guitar? The answer to both questions: Of course not.

Both Mike and Bill work with people, which means they have to have at least a little...um, talent.

They have co-workers, managers, and employees. Mike might not think about the folks he works with in those terms, but that's what they are. His fellow band mates are co-workers, the band has a manager, and the folks that help them put on the show are employees – whether they're working for cash, free beer, or the chance to be a part of something cool.

As I said earlier, business is nothing but exchanges, and that's what working for cash, free beer, or clout is all about. It's also about exchanging work for work. Both Bill and Mike put their time and efforts into the bank and band respectively because others are doing the same. They are literally exchanging work because they know it is creating something bigger than their efforts would create alone.

Questions:
1. Who are some of the key people in your music career?
2. Can you label them as co-workers, managers or employees?
3. Is there an overlap?
4. Is it hard to think of some of these people in these ways?

A Life

"Mike and Bill both go inside and watch the news while they eat dinner. At 7:45 Mike changes into his stage outfit – a pair of torn jeans and a tee shirt – checks his hair and heads off to pick up his girlfriend on the way to the gig. Bill changes clothes, calls his girlfriend and makes plans for lunch tomorrow. He then sits back and settles in for a night of ESPN."

Mike and Bill have homes, girlfriends, and a little free time. They each have a life.

In addition to the struggle with work and identity I mentioned earlier, many artists also struggle to separate work from their lives. While this is easy to understand given the nature of "making art for a living," that doesn't lessen the dangers.

Despite your love for practicing, rehearsing, and making art, you need to recognize how draining these activities can be, especially considering your intimate involvement with your craft. Despite what you may think, you can't go on being drained without eventually becoming empty, and emptiness is not a pretty thing. Why do you think so many artists struggle with mind-numbing addictions?

It's also possible that you don't want what you think you do. It's possible that while you think you want to be an international star and tour the world, what you truly desire is to express yourself and travel the world. If this is the case, the international star part is nothing more than a means to an end. You might be more satisfied creating art while teaching English as a second language in major cities all over the world. Same result, different means.

Questions:
1. Do you ever feel emotionally drained?
2. What do you do about it?
3. Have you ever separated the things you want from life from the things you want from your career?
4. Who are some of the key people in your life?
5. Are these some of the people you listed as co-workers, managers or employees?
6. Do you think that's a good thing or a bad thing?

Customers

Finally, in contemplating the merger of the bank and the recording deal for the band, Mike says that the label can "get us out to the media and the fans we need" and Bill's merger will "bring a larger customer base to our operation and the more attention we get the better it is for business."

Customers are the life blood of all business.

If you are going to make a living in the arts, you have to come to the realization that you will be dependent on customers. By definition that means people who not only like what you do, but actually pay you to do it. These payments might be direct, as in the form of buying your work, or indirect by turning their friends into fans that buy your work.

Questions:
1. Who are your customers?
2. Is it hard to think of these people as customers?
3. Is that a good or bad thing?
4. Are some of them also your co-workers?

Talent is NOT Enough

Don't misunderstand anything I've said as diminishing the importance of talent. Talent, and the honing of your talent over years and years of work, is critical to your success in the arts.

On the other hand, don't diminish the importance of what I'm saying about treating the creative arts as a job. Success will remain just out of reach as long as you rely solely on talent to build and sustain your career. It'll be out of reach because you will never invest in the tools, clothes, concepts, skills, perspective and relationships necessary for success.

"Give me six hours to chop down a tree and I will spend the first four sharpening the axe."

~ **Abraham Lincoln**

And it will stay out of reach because you'll never recognize you don't have enough talent.

CHAPTER 2

I THOUGHT I HAD ENOUGH TALENT

I performed for my 3rd grade class and I had the kids in the palm of my hand.

As I gradually increased the speed of my sticks, the sound became a blur. With every eye fixed on me, I began to enjoy the moment. "Even the jocks who pick on me are watching," I thought.

The girls were watching too.

I was the kid who hit things all the time. Since I had the benefit of being born into a musical family, it wasn't long before my mother declared, "We have a drummer on our hands." Despite my skeptical dad, I soon had a toy drum. I have a photograph of me playing that drum on my mom's knee while she played a wooden flute.

I was two.

As I got a little older, I graduated to what could loosely be called a drum set. It came from Sears and was made mostly of cardboard. That was followed on my 6th birthday by my first real drum set - it had an orange sparkle finish.

I had arrived!

It wasn't long before I was putting on concerts and performances for neighborhood kids. Our home movies show my friends excitedly watching as I played along with a record at a birthday party. Looking back I'm sure they were bored out of their minds, but I thought they were excited at the time.

My childhood was spent playing with every music group I could find, in and out of school. When the time came to decide what I was going to do for a career, it was more like a decision that didn't need to be made - I had the talent to play music, so I would be a professional musician.

And it worked.

After high school, I attended the University Of North Texas. I went for its world-renowned jazz education program and a chance to compete against some of the best musicians in the country. I practiced everyday, worked my way up the ranks, and got quite a bit of attention there and in the Dallas/Fort Worth music scene as well.

After graduation, I stayed in Texas playing sessions and clubs with various bands - one of which had a lovely singer who soon became my wife. The same year we were married, I auditioned for and got the gig with the Contemporary Christian artist Russ Taff. That's what brought us to Nashville in 1987.

I continued to have success after we moved, too. Russ worked on and off throughout the year so I had time to play with other folks in the studio, locally, and on the road. I was the hot new kid in town and work came easily.

For a while.

Eventually my career leveled off. I worked, but I never got rich. I played with great people, but never with huge stars. I made a living, but didn't build a long term career.

I failed in the creative arts because I didn't have enough talent.

Self-development – you can learn it all

Based on that experience, I give you the pivotal question of the book: *Are you the best in the world at what you do?*

It's a pivotal question because your answer determines every aspect of how you're approaching your career. It's also pivotal because if you're like me, you've never been asked it before. I'm not saying you haven't thought about this question though, because if you are honest, you have. Often.

There have been countless times you've seen or heard someone's work or performance and thought, "Crap! They're amazing! I hope no one ever compares me to them." Or, "WOW, how will I ever get any work if I have to do what THEY do?" Or the classic, "I'm glad they don't live in my town!"

I know, because I have thought all three of those and more. I even joked about it with friends in college. Anytime we were blown away by some amazing drummer, my buddy Pete and I would grab each other's foot and pretend we were shoe salesmen. There we were in a concert hall in Dallas asking, "Would you like to see this in an 8 ½ or 9?" Yeah, funny.

Yes, the question about talent was on my mind, just like it's been on yours, but no one made us stop and answer the question. Until now. So, are you the best in the world at what you do?

I'll answer for you: No, you are not. Now, before you get all defensive, let me explain my answer.

First, I say, "No," because we can't define "the best." It's not enough to say "The best writer, dancer, or artist in the world." For instance, what kind of artist? Painter? Sculptor? Architect? And what kind of art? Modern? Classic? Impressionist?

Second, I say, "No," because "the best" is subjective - just like all art is subjective. Do you know of any two people who have the exact same taste in art? Me neither.

Third, even if you perfectly define "the best," and find that everyone has the exact same taste in the art you love, the answer's still (probably), "No." Why? Because we live in a BIG interconnected world and you now must compete on a global scale. Odds are that there's someone somewhere that makes what you do look bad in comparison.

> ...nothing is more common
>
> than unsuccessful
>
> people with talent.
>
> ~ **Calvin Coolidge**

Just sayin.'

And fourth, you're wasting your time answering this question because talent doesn't matter anyway.

Fairness

My hunch is that you're freakin' out right now because you believe that only the exceptionally talented should be stars and everyone else should go home. In support of this belief you can point to a long list of exceptionally talented stars. Well, I have a list like that, too, and I agree that talented people may indeed become stars.

However, I suggest that for every exceptionally talented star there are three or four UN-talented stars, and 30 or 40 people you've never heard of that are twice as good as the star. There it is: a non-scientific statistic that says relying on talent alone gives you 1 in 44 chance of making it. I'll go one step further and say that even the exceptionally talented stars didn't make it on talent alone (and you'll see examples throughout this book).

Is this fair? Well, it depends on your definition of fair. If by fair you mean that the creative arts should reward only the most gifted people on the planet, then no, it's not fair. On the other hand, if you believe the arts should reward the most gifted, relational, business and marketing savvy, self-confident, and mature individuals possible, then yes, it's fair.

I'm hammering this point hard because it's so crucial to your success. How you answer "Are you the best in the world," and what you DO with your answer drives and supports your approach to your life and career.

> As long as you have certain desires about how it ought to be you can't see how it is.-
>
> ~ Ram Dass

If you believe you are better than everyone else at what you do, you will gravitate towards, and surround yourself with, those who believe likewise. You will also shun anyone who offers the slightest bit of criticism – whether it's legitimate or not. Over time, two things will happen. One, you will stagnate creatively because of a self-centered feedback loop that says nothing but "You're the best!" Two, you will become increasingly fixated on proving you're the best to those who don't believe. You'll die frustrated and bitter.

If you believe you are not the best in the world, you have four choices:

1. You can quit now and go sell shoes. And maybe you should quit. Seriously. I've met LOTS of creatives who wasted their lives chasing fortune and fame. Most of them were supported by the people I mentioned above, the ones shouting "You're the best, you're the best!" They weren't the best and they KNEW they weren't, but they didn't have the heart or guts to say ENOUGH!

2. You can double your efforts to become the best in the world. This is a choice that's common and understandable, but not recommend because of the simple fact that it leads you into the "die frustrated and bitter" life just described.
3. You can think this is a dumb question and ignore it, like I did.
4. You can wake up to the fact that your long term career success does not depend on being the best and devote yourself to learning what does.

I recommend you choose number 4.

Combinations

It's easy to assume that what's needed in "The Arts" is creative talent and what's needed in the "Real World" is technical skill. But is that really true? I suggest what's needed in both worlds is a combination of both. I have met gifted musicians who could not play with a band because they never practiced. I have also worked with musicians of average talent that are tremendous players because they've worked their tails off. The same thing can be said of dancers, photographers, actors, writers and producers.

But, what about outside of the arts? Is a combination of skill and talent needed there, too?

Consider doctors. If you need brain surgery, would you want the most experienced surgeon, the one with the most natural talent, or the one who was the appropriate blend of both? I would pick an experienced and creative surgeon; one that had spent years gaining the necessary knowledge and skills, and who also had the talent for using split second creativity and improvisational skills to save lives during surgery.

Wouldn't you choose the same guy?

Music, and all art, has rules and regulations and structure just like other fields do, and that fact must be dealt with correctly and respectfully. Think about what would have happened if I had played heavy-metal drums with The Sweethearts of the Rodeo. Would you say I was being creative, or should I get fired? What about vice-a-versa (country drums with The Demons of the Rodeo)? Fired also, right?

My point is that "The Arts" is not all about freedom of expression, and the "Real World" is not all about rules and regulations. When I put a band together for a project I look for the same qualities in the musicians that I would want in my doctor, mechanic, or financial advisor. I want a band full of folks that know the rules AND can create fresh music at the same time.

It's also important to note the importance of creativity and skills in areas beyond career specifics, regardless of whether you are a brain surgeon or an actor. We want our brain surgeon to be creative and skilled in the operating room, but we'd also like him to have a great bedside manner. A clean office with a pleasant and well trained staff and an ability to properly track our payments would be nice as well. It would also help if he was a capable marketer, so you could actually find him when you needed brain surgery.

Soft Skills

The difference between failure and success in the arts and the real world will always come down to combinations of what is known as "hard skills" and "soft skills."

Hard skills are the technical skills needed to do a job. Things like proper form for dancers, brush techniques for painters, and comedic timing for actors. Soft skills are things like communication, listening, networking, etc.

It may surprise you to learn which skills are more important.

- Harvard University research states that long-term career achievements are 80% determined by soft skills and only 20% determined by hard skills.

- Research conducted with Fortune 500 CEOs by the Stanford Research Institute International and the Carnegie Melon Foundation found that 75 percent of long-term job success depends on people skills, while only 25 percent depends on technical knowledge.

- Indiana Business Research Center (IBRC) discovered that, while credentialing in the form of degrees and certificates is important, development of soft skills - skills that are more social than technical - are a crucial part of fostering a dynamic workforce. Skills projected to be in the highest demand for all Indiana occupations through 2014 include active listening, critical thinking, speaking, active learning, writing, time management, and social perceptiveness.

- In a Job Outlook 2008 survey conducted by the National Association of Colleges & Employers (NACE), the top characteristics looked for in new hires by 276 employer respondents (mostly from the service sector) were all soft skills: communication ability, a strong work ethic, initiative, interpersonal skills, and teamwork.

Can We Learn More?

I hope by now you have arrived at the conclusion that there are no differences between people in "The Arts" and the "Real World." I also hope that you have begun to think just a little bit differently about yourself and your career in the creative arts.

It's time for us to begin exploring all the "Real World" knowledge I wish I had known about when I was in "The Arts." Let's look over the wall I spoke of earlier and see how business people approach all the topics we just covered. We'll begin with the most important of all the soft skills: people.

CHAPTER 3

THE COMPANY I KEPT

It was a typical night on the road.

A bunch of us musicians sat and talked while traveling on a bus from one city to the next. On this particular night, we were complaining about the stupidity of the song, "Achy Breaky Heart," and the stupidity of Billy Ray Cyrus fans everywhere (my apologies if you happen to be a Billy Ray Cyrus fan).

At the time, I was touring with Wayne Massey and Charlie McClain, a husband and wife duo famous for their work on soap operas (Wayne) and country music (Charlie). The year before I toured with them, Billy

Ray Cyrus had exploded onto the country music scene into instant stardom. All because of that stupid song.

Wayne overheard our conversation and stopped us in our tracks. He simply, but passionately, said that it didn't matter what we thought. Whether we liked it or not, Billy Ray Cyrus had made 16 million people spend their hard-earned money for his music, and he was therefore a valid artist and a success in the entertainment industry.

We had to admit he was right, and that wasn't the only time. Wayne set us straight on lots of things while we worked together. He had a different perspective and enjoyed sharing it with us - whether we wanted to hear it or not.

I can't say for sure whether we wanted to hear what he had to say or not. What I do know is that when we were alone, all we talked about was how we thought he was wrong. It was as if we were encouraging each other to stick with what we knew, instead of daring to think differently.

But at the end of each trip, we would happily go home to our little homes in our little cars while Wayne and Charlie drove their $750,000 bus to their mansion.

I failed in the creative arts because of the company I kept.

You can't do it alone – networking and crabs in a bucket

People

People matter, and not just in the family and friend sense, either. They matter for your career. As in my Billy Ray Cyrus story, who you hang around will affect you, whether you know it or not. The way they affect you will, in turn, affect your career.

I can understand how you might think I was stupid. I prefer to think I was blind. Blinded by my "I have enough talent to work" perception, I remained ignorant to the evidence all around me. That is why I spent most of the last chapter pushing you to lose your "Talent is all that matters" perception, too. I speak from experience when I say it is crucial to understand that talent is only part of the equation, and maybe not even the biggest part.

While I'm talking about perceptions, let me clarify that, yes, I am saying you should make friends to get work. Isn't that sacrilegious or illegal or something? I mean, isn't that USING PEOPLE? Well, consider the alternative.

You are no longer allowed to:
- Work with anyone you like or share common interests with.
- Work with any individual you met anywhere outside of your creative endeavors or those with which you share common artistic or life interests.
- Work with any individual more than once because a friendship might develop.

Sound okay to you?

Using People

My Nashville music career:

1. While living in Dallas, I got a call from a friend saying she had heard Russ Taff was holding auditions. I tracked down the management numbers and got an audition. I made the band and met the late Jackie Street among many others.
2. Jackie got me work at Hummingbird Studios, an advertising music production company in Nashville. This led to other "jingle" work (TV and Radio commercials) as well as custom recording projects.
3. During a break from touring with Russ, Jackie was asked to play for Paul Smith, another Contemporary Christian singer. He asked me to play drums. Among others in the band, I met guitarist Dennis Dearing.
4. Dennis worked with several writers at Benson Music (a publishing company and record label). He got me work with these writers which led to countless custom projects over the years.
5. Jackie also played in a rock band that needed a drummer and I met Michael Cody, Gene Ford, and Mark Chesshir. I joined the band (one of the best bands I've ever been in, and one that went nowhere). Mark is one of our dearest friends to this day.
6. Mark hired me for countless demos and projects he worked on over the years.
7. One of the demo projects involved a talented couple named Scott and Christine Dente that later became Out of the Grey.
8. Their demo led to their recording contract. I played on their debut CD.

I could go on and on, but you get the point: I can track every job - including when I left the music industry - to Jackie Street.

Exchanges

At the time the Gibson/Miller Band came together, Dave Gibson – the lead vocalist & acoustic guitar player – was enjoying the life of a successful songwriter. He had written several huge hits, was making a strong six-figure income and had even won the CMA Song of the Year Award. For quite a while it seemed every singer in Nashville was recording a song written by Dave.

Like most successful songwriters, Dave had a contract with a music publishing company in Nashville. A publishing company is a business that assists songwriters with the legal, financial, and business side of songwriting. They take care of all the copyrighting and licensing paperwork and fees. They collect and distribute funds, called royalties, and help writers get their songs recorded through a process known as "pitching."

Pitching, or plugging, is the process of getting songs into the hands of people who choose music for singers, music projects, commercials, TV shows, and movies. It's the primary activity of publishing companies and they have staffs of employees whose sole responsibility is plugging songs to producers and artists in hopes of getting a song recorded.

If you're not familiar with this business, you might be asking yourself why these companies exist and how they make money. If you'll recall, in Chapter One I wrote that business is simple if you think of it terms of exchanges. Let's apply that thinking here and see what's being exchanged and why.

Dave wrote songs and still does; great songs. But great songs are a dime a dozen (no disrespect to Dave), and most never get heard by anyone. Dave partners with a publishing company because they have staffs of employees whose sole responsibility is plugging songs to producers and artists in hopes of getting a song recorded.
When that recording makes money, guess what happens? The publishing company keeps a percentage of the profits for their time, efforts, and expertise.

But here's the kicker: one night while the band was riding on the bus between shows, Dave was telling us about his career, the hits he had written, and related events when he said, "I never got a cut that I didn't pitch myself."

He went on to explain that no matter how good the people were that worked as song pluggers, nothing could take the place of networking and performing the songs live. He explained that every cut he had gotten had come from a conversation between friends after he sang a song in a Nashville club.

While this apparently negates the need for an exchange of any kind, it still makes sense if we dig deeper. An important detail I've left off is the fact that songwriters like Dave get paid by publishing companies before the songs are recorded. Songwriters get a monthly salary in exchange for agreeing to write a specific number of songs each year. In effect, the songwriter gets paid to write full time in return for a percentage of future royalties. If none of their songs ever get recorded, they still get paid.

So how and why does a publishing company assume this risk? The "how" is accomplished by controlling the risks, and the biggest risk is the songwriters themselves. Publishing companies concentrate much of their efforts on signing the best and brightest songwriters they can find, as well as signing songwriters in various stages of their careers: new, established and retiring.

New songwriters are the riskiest, but can also have the biggest reward. They are risky because they are an unknown in terms of both their ability to write hit songs and their name recognition. They are potentially the most rewarding because they have their whole career ahead of them and they don't need much money. They are often young and happy to earn ANY money at all, so the publishers don't have to pay them much per month.

Established songwriters, like Dave, have a track record of hit songs and a name recognition that publishers love. On the royalty side, this means it's likely that money will be made in the future. On the pay side (to the songwriter) it can go one of two ways: high or low. Signing a successful songwriter can be high cost because of their prior success. It can also be low because they already have a continuous stream of royalties coming in from years of writing hit songs and they don't need a monthly salary. They simply like the song plugging (more on that in a sec), licensing and royalty administration assistance the publishing company provides, and gladly give them a percentage of future royalties in exchange.

Retiring songwriters include those that are slowing down or ready to "sell out" completely. Those that are slowing down have the track record and name recognition, as do those ready to quit. Both have catalogs. A catalog is the collection of songs written by someone over their career, over a specific time frame. Publishing companies often buy catalogs outright by paying the writer a flat fee – sometimes large, sometimes not so large. In exchange, they become the sole recipient of all future royalties.

Another way the publishing companies mitigate risk is the previously discussed "staffs of employees whose sole responsibility is plugging songs to producers and artists in hopes of getting a song recorded." Despite Dave's comment to the contrary, pluggers are the back bone of the publishing industry. Even he'd admit that it's likely those people he talked to in clubs had already heard his songs once or twice because of the pluggers.

Now we come to the "why," and it's an easy answer: money. You knew that, right? Of course you did because you paid attention to my statement that "you are pursuing a career in an industry every bit as much as Henry Ford did a century ago."

But I'd do us both a disservice if I left you with the impression that this is all about money, because it's not. It's about people. In the world of business people are called customers, and there's only one way to deal with customers: serve them.

Customers 101

Let's go back to the story of Bill and Mike to learn more because they both understood the hidden power of their pending deals.

Bill and his bank were excited about their merger, and Mike and his band were also excited about their record deal, right? Why? Because both plans brought the guys and their co-workers more customers. When you cut through all of the hype of mergers, acquisitions, and contracts, you'll find that this is often the case.

The press releases would be filled with talk of 'synergies' and 'team work' but what's truly going on is the fact that a merger can often double a company's customer base overnight. Just this past year, Wachovia and Wells Fargo merged their banks (or Wells bought them up). My wife and I were customers of Wachovia, we're now customers of Wells Fargo. Virtually overnight.

The same is true of our example of Mike and his band's recording contract. Just like the hype surrounding mergers and acquisitions, what's really going on with all record contracts is customer acquisition. Like Bill's bank, we can assume that Mike and his band have a decent sized fan base (customers) or the record company wouldn't be talking with them at all. The record label, through its distribution channels, sales people, and other similar musical artists, has access to thousands or millions of fans. Put them together and everyone wins.

This is what I meant when I said you couldn't earn a living alone. Whether alone or in partnership with others, the ability to reach and connect with customers is critical. Connection is the key. You have to find a way to touch people deeply enough that they will pay for that touch. Since art is appreciated in many different ways, this can be a gray area, but don't let that confuse what I'm trying to relate to you. There are billions of people to serve in the world and we'll talk more about customers later.

My point here is the importance of people. Both Mike and Bill worked with people and their "mergers" were also about people. Dave's success as a songwriter was a result of people - people he knew through his networking, and singing, and those that pitched songs for the publishing company. Your success will be the result of the people you know, too.

The Power of Association

Though I don't have personal experience, I'm told that crab hunting is quite an adventure. You and your friends grab some buckets and wade out into the water to seek your prey. Once found, you simply pick them up and put them in the bucket.

There's one small problem that causes the adventure: runaway crabs. Evidently, if you put one crab in the bucket, it will quickly and easily climb out and run away. The solution? put two or more crabs in the bucket. When one of them begins to climb out, the others grab hold and pull them back in.

Just like people.

The story about the band members and me at the beginning of this chapter is a story about crabs in a bucket. It wasn't that we meant to keep each other in the bucket of barely surviving musicians, but that's what we did.

We kept each other in the bucket by grabbing each other's ideas instead of Wayne's because we were comfortable with our ideas and we knew they worked. Maybe not in a big way, but small success is better than no success. Wayne's ideas, on the other hand, were new, unproven to us, and therefore scary.

Our conversations were full of comments like, "Yeah, that's a great idea, but..." or, "I tried to do that once, but..."

The word "but" is used all the time in crab-in-a-bucket conversations and it's always followed with something like "it won't work." What they are really saying is, "It didn't work for me and therefore it can't possibly work for you either, so don't even try."

I titled this chapter "The Company I Kept" because I've realized I hung out with crabs. Oh, they were wonderful people; dear friends in fact, but they were crabs nonetheless (And by the way, if you're a friend who's reading this, I'm talking about my 'other' friends).

All kidding aside, let me say this another way: If I want to learn about you, your current life, and where you'll be in five years, all I have to do is meet 10 or 12 of your friends. Your life is essentially identical to theirs in terms of where you live, and what you do, and your income is the same, give or take 15%.

If you all stick together, the same will be true in 5 years.

The same was true of me. I hung around people that were just like me – struggling creatives trying to figure out how to make it in the arts. Our crabbiness came out when one of us had a different idea, because it would invariably be questioned (or shot down completely) by someone else in conversations like this:

Me: "Sometimes I think I should just raise my rates because it'll seem like I work more and I'll get more calls. Plus, I'll cut down on some of the time wasting work. Whatchya think?"

Friend(s): "Hmmm. I heard that worked for Mike B., but he blah, blah, blah, blah..." - *It really doesn't matter WHAT was said, what matters is that the answer had the word 'but' in it.*

Me: "Yeah, that's true."

So I skipped that idea with a sigh of relief that I hadn't done something foolish.

By the way, Mike B. was a first call, A-list bass player. He played on close to half of the hit records at that time, partly because he raised his fees at a turning point in his career. He's still first call.

That's real life crabs in a buckets, and that's the power of association.

Please understand that these were not crabby people. They weren't trying to hold back my career, or theirs. They wanted to succeed as badly as I did. The problem was none of us knew how. How could we?

Just like actual crabs in a bucket, we all only knew one thing: to grab at anything that was moving and hold on tight. Little did we know that the grabbing was actually keeping us from the success we desired.

Contrast this with the story of Gretchen Williams. A singer/songwriter country music star who enjoyed a meteoric rise to fame. Her smash debut album exploded on the scene powered by the single, "Red Neck Woman."

Long before that "meteoric rise" she had worked her guts out as a singer/songwriter in Nashville for at least 10 years. I read in an interview with her, about how she met John Rich, of the country duo Big and Rich, in a club when she first moved to town. She credits him with helping her successfully navigate the music business.
They also co-wrote "Red Neck Woman."

Again, the power of association.

Now, I'm not suggesting you dump your friends. I'm suggesting you recognize that they are not your best source for career advice due to the simple fact that they don't know any more than you do.

The same goes for family, too. If Auntie May says you're the most awesome entertainer the world has ever known, ask yourself this question: Who was the last successful artist Auntie May signed to a multi-million dollar contract?

I suggest you consciously think about the people with whom you spend your time. Are they supportive of you and your dreams? Are they heading in the same direction as you? Are some of them at a place in their lives where you want to be – slightly and/or way ahead of you in terms of career, family, life, etc.? If you can answer, "Yes," make it a point to spend time with these people regularly.

If you don't have people like this, find some. Call them up and say you'd like to spend time with them and learn what they know about whatever it is you want to learn about. Be clear and candid and tell them exactly what you're after. Most will be flattered that you're asking and will be glad to help.

Two things to keep in mind about these "mentoring" relationships. First, they _are_ relationships. Be yourself and work at having a friendship. If that doesn't happen, find someone else. Second, reciprocate in some way. If it's a more formal mentorship, buy them meals for their time. Less formal relationships will naturally reciprocate over time.

Recap

So, how are we doing so far?

- Do you know you can't "make it" on talent alone?
- Do you know that's a good thing, because you don't have enough talent anyway?
- Do you know you can learn anything and everything you need to find your success?
- Yes, you?
- Do you know you have a unique combination of talents, skills, and interests?
- Do you know that success is often less about abilities and more about people skills?
- Do you know that you need people to succeed?
- Customers?
- Do you know how to identify and avoid crabs in a bucket?
- Do you agree that there is little difference between "The Arts" and the "Real World?"

No matter your answers, we're going to push forward. I'm confident that as we dig deep into the real world of business, the answers will become clearer. *Your* answers will become clearer.

Now we're going to look at the kinds of people who start and run businesses. They are fascinating individuals that can be divided into two categories: successful and un-successful.

Just like some creatives I know...

CHAPTER 4

HOW I KEPT MY COMPANY

FAILED

I created my first newsletter in 1992 when I was in the Gibson/Miller Band.

I'm not sure what gave me the idea, but I decided to create and send a monthly news sheet about the things I had going on. Every month I'd type - on a typewriter - short blurbs about gigs the band played, sessions I had recorded and general updates about my career. I used a copier to resize and combine the blurbs into a two-sided sheet I could fold and mail to my readers - Nashville music producers, the band's management and label people, my endorsement folks, other musicians, and some of the band's fans if they asked for it.

I had two reasons for doing this newsletter: the first was to help push the career of the band by adding to the publicity buzz in a small, but personal way. The second was to keep myself in the minds of the readers that could hire me when I was home. I was marketing myself.

That newsletter was one of the only times I acted as if I was in business for myself. It was one of the only times I marketed, planned, and managed the things I was doing outside of drumming.

What's important to understand though, is that whether I realized it or not, I was marketing, planning, and managing all time; badly. My lack of knowledge about it just meant I was like a company with a killer product and awful commercials; a failure.

I failed in the creative arts because of how I kept my company.

You own a business and it's YOU!

Businesses and the People Who Start Them

Businesses are started and run by people...and that's where the trouble begins.

Have you ever heard the statistic that 80% of new businesses fail within the first five years? It gets worse. 80% of the remaining 20% fail in the next 5 years!

Why do I bring up such a sad statistic?

Is it so you'll be glad you're an artist and not a business owner? No. I bring it up because the reasons why most businesses fail hold huge lessons for people in the arts.

I Quit!

Most businesses are started by people who hate their boss. They find themselves at work one day saying, "That's it. I've had it! I hate getting ordered around by a man (or woman) that can't do half what I can. In fact, I'll bet I could make twice as much money doing this on my own and I wouldn't have to split the profits with that (insert expletive here). I'm OUTTA HERE!!!"

So, they start a business doing whatever it is they do. For conversation sake, let's call them "Doers." Doers often succeed at first because they are quite good at what they do and they thrive on their new-found independence. But problems in their business arise because they *are* the business, and it's not really a business.

Because they are the business, everything works fine until success starts to come and there's too much work for them to handle. Without anyone else to rely on, Doers quickly start to burn out. Of course they try to keep up, but inevitably they are caught between two choices: give up and close the business, or slow the business down to a manageable level of activity. That "manageable level" is simply how much work they can accomplish in however many hours they can work each day.

This is why it's not really a business. By definition a business is a systematic approach to supplying goods or services. The word system is important because a business should establish teams and/or processes that can run without the owner's input. In fact, a characteristic of a true business is that the owner can sell it to someone else.

What I've described above fails this test and is actually nothing more than a job that's owned and managed by the Doer. This is common with Doers because they like to do and they lack the skills necessary to build a true business. They also don't like to give up control, so they don't.

People in "The Arts" are, for the most part, Doers.

Imagine This!

Other people start businesses because they have a grand vision of accomplishing something. These people are "Dreamers." They are true visionaries. Dreamers are rare, but they do exist. The challenge for these people is that by nature, they do a lot of dreaming and not much doing. They have the plans and the courage to start, but fail to follow through on the execution required to be successful.

These people also don't like the day-to-day organizing and managing that a business requires. They don't like being bugged by details and would rather concentrate on the grandiose plans for the future. They also often lack the discipline necessary to build and nurture relationships, which causes difficulties when they need other people's help (and remember, we all need people to succeed). Dreamers believe in the power of their dreams and don't see the point in anything else. Creatives are also often Dreamers. Like those I know who are always waiting for the 'perfect' gig.

And speaking of perfect:

It Has To Be Perfect!

The last category of people who start businesses is made up of people who are good at details. These "Detailers" have charts and graphs and plans for every task that must be performed. They are extremely good at organizing and finishing things, as well as managing people to organize and finish.

This group is similar to the Doers. They quit jobs in a huff and start companies, but they don't do it out of a desire for independence. Detailers start companies because they want to do it better. They start businesses around "perfect products" or "perfect services" and just like the Doers, it works! Or, it works until they have too much work to do and they have to hire employees. Then their drive for perfection causes them to micro-manage every last detail to the point where it hurts productivity and the morale of everyone involved.

And My Point Is?

The reason 80% of businesses fail is because they are started and run by these people. The Doer does great things, but because they don't plan for growth, won't give control, and can't keep up with growing demand, their business is doomed to fail. The Dreamer envisions wonderful solutions to the problems of his fellow man, but is not good at following through or organizing the necessary day-to-day tasks. The Detailer drives everyone away with a relentless pursuit of perfection!

These are the same reasons artists fail.

The majority of artists are Doers who think their talent makes them the best at "doing." They practice and practice and know every possible way to impress other artists and the public alike. They often think their way is the best way, and that they are better than other artists. While working in one situation, they are usually looking for a better gig so they can work with better Doers.

Then there are the Dreamers; true "artists" whose talent is truly stunning. Wherever they go, people fawn all over them. They are eternally dissatisfied and unreliable and never seem to "get it together."

Finally, there are our Detailers. The artists that are meticulously detailed in all that they do. If you want it right and on time, you call them. But if you want passion and heart, you'll often come up empty. These people work, but they rarely have the drive or flash that leads to success and they constantly criticize everyone else.

So what's the answer? Learn to become all three.

Doer + Dreamer + Detailer = Success

Think of any successful company and think about how it works. The company "does" its product or service well by offering excellent design and/or construction that's viable in the marketplace.

It has a dream, a clear vision of why it exists. It knows where it's headed in the future and it has the ability to communicate this message effectively.

It organizes and manages itself well. By that I mean it accomplishes the logistical tasks surrounding its product and/or service successfully and handles problems and growth efficiently and properly.

Now I ask you, what would happen if you functioned the same way?

Imagine the life you'd have if you were accomplished at your craft, had a reason for what you do, and managed all the details well.

You would:
- Make exceptional art when it counts, every time.
- Know why you exist and where you want to go
- Communicate this message through everything you do.
- Relate to people in such a way as to attract work and the customers to support that work.
- Organize yourself around this purpose and manage yourself well by handling all the logistical tasks surrounding your life so your product and service is delivered successfully while you handle problems and career growth efficiently and consistently.

You Own A Business, And It's You!

"You own a business, and it's you" may seem like a cute little title for this section, but I assure you I mean these words and all they imply. This statement will serve to direct and focus your professional goals. It will also frame discussions about interactions and integrations you will have with other artists and consumers as well as the true businesses that make up the artistic industries.

The message I continue to hammer home is that most artist's approach to their career is based on their talents and abilities. You now know that perspective is inadequate at best. "You own a business, and it's you" helps, but I know it's not that simple.

When you express yourself through your art, you are...well...expressing yourself through your art. You literally reveal and expose intimate parts of your thoughts and emotions through what you do. This is what makes it so fulfilling. Please don't take anything I say in this book as discounting that fact. Having lived 20 years in "The Arts," I know how deeply moving this profession can be. I hope you love it with a passion as I did (and still do).

But this passion often leads to the confusion I personally experienced in my career, and confusion always causes one of two responses: inactivity or random activity. Inactivity is self-explanatory; people who are confused just stop. Those that don't stop launch into random activity – doing anything and everything harder than ever before - and by now we know what that looks like for musicians.

To combat your struggle I offer you the "you own a business" statement here. Its purpose is to help define elements of your life and career into distinct categories as a guard against confusion. By saying you own a business you can step back from yourself and treat every decision you make as if you were an entrepreneur managing a business.

You, Inc.

Building on the statement that you own a business, consider the following list:
- You, Inc. needs a mission.
- You, Inc. needs a board of directors.
- You, Inc. needs a product.
- You, Inc. needs goals.
- You, Inc. needs a business plan.
- You, Inc. needs a marketing strategy.
- You, Inc. needs customers.
- You, Inc. needs a sales team.
- You, Inc. needs capital.
- You, Inc. needs to be profitable.
- You, Inc. needs a building.

You, Inc. needs a nap....

Exhausting? Sure. Can you do it? Yes.

Let's dive into basic definitions and thoughts that we'll explore in more detail later.

A Business

Since we've just agreed you own a business, and we've given this company a name - You, Inc. - let's define what we mean:

A business is a person or organization that has the legal standing to enter into a contract, take on an obligation, and assume responsibility for its actions. - The American Heritage Dictionary of Business Terms

Dictionary.com defines a business more simply as "A person, partnership or corporation engaged in commerce, manufacturing or a service."

These definitions describe you as a musician:

- You pay taxes, right? That means you have legal standing as a person.
- You can, and do, enter into contracts (written or spoken), take on obligations and assume responsibility for your actions.
- Your art, no matter what form its in, allows you to engage in commerce, manufacturing or service.

You own a business, and it's you. Congratulations, let's get to work.

A Mission

A mission is the reason why a company exists. It is the most important part of running a business. It is also one of the hardest things to put together, so we'll cover Mission in greater depth in future chapters.

A Board of Directors

When I made my living in the music business, the concept of a board of directors was a mystery to me. I envisioned groups of cigar smoking men having secret handshakes when they met. They attended closed door meetings around long oak tables with lots of yelling and wrangling as million dollar decisions were made and ratified. Then the doors would open and the group would solemnly file out into the world, sworn to secrecy on the threat of death.

I've come to realize that a board of directors is an official, organized group of advisors; nothing more and nothing less. A good board will have people from diverse backgrounds and areas of expertise that can assist the person (or persons) leading a company as they contemplate important matters.

> I don't know everything. But I can find out anything within five minutes.
>
> - Henry Ford

Sounds a lot like the group of people we discussed in the last chapter doesn't it? That's why I brought it up. You need to consciously assemble a group of trusted advisors if you have any hope for success. As Robert Kiyosaki says, "Success is a team sport." So, who's on your team?

Whether or not you decide to meet formally doesn't matter. What matters is that you understand the importance of who is on your board, why they are on your board, and that you get around them regularly and often.

You, Inc. Needs a Product

We had been asked to come to the Sony Record's offices on Music Row in Nashville to view the results of the photo shoot for our second project. My Gibson/Miller Band mates and I quickly agreed on 10 or 15 pictures that we wanted to see as part of our second release, "Red,

White and Blue Collar." We left the offices excited about the photos that perfectly captured a bunch of guys who loved to play and have fun.

A month or two later, the record label executive assigned to our project traveled to meet us on the road and show us the preliminary layouts for our CD's, tapes, and posters. Noticeably missing were ANY of the images we had selected as a band. We were incredulous and more than a bit frustrated! When we demanded to know what happened, he simply stated there weren't any other photos that were acceptable.

Huh?

In our hotel room the next day, the bass player and I discussed the whole situation. I was dumbfounded. I knew we had chosen many great pictures for our project. The bass player's reply? "We're just soap on a shelf."

I was stunned by what he said. It felt awful to think that my blood, sweat, and tears; my life's dream and passion; my life's work was being compared to soap on a shelf in a supermarket!

But, I soon began to admit he was right. Our music, and everything attached to it, was simply the product Sony was packaging, promoting and selling at the time. It didn't matter what we did or didn't think; we were being marketed and sold to support Sony's goals, plans, and dreams.

You Are Just Soap On A Shelf

Every business has something it offers to the public. Whether it is a product or a service, expensive or cheap, a necessity or luxury really doesn't matter. All that matters is the concept of exchange, which means the product or service must be something someone wants and is willing to pay for.

My question to you, Mr. or Ms. CEO of You, Inc. is: What is your product? What is it that you offer to the world? What kind of soap is it? How will it compete against the other soaps? Why will people choose it off the shelf? How will it be seen on the shelf so it CAN be chosen?

Note the words "...my question to you Mr. or Ms. CEO of You, Inc." Next to your company's mission statement, your product decisions are the most important you'll make. I encourage you to approach them with the objectivity of a business owner instead of the personally invested artist you are. Here's how:

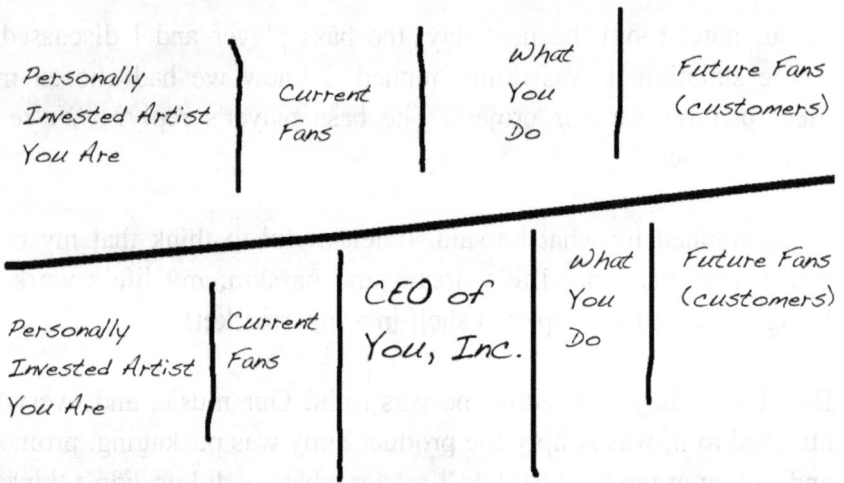

Personally Invested Artist You Are	Current Fans		What You Do	Future Fans (customers)
Personally Invested Artist You Are	Current Fans	CEO of You, Inc.	What You Do	Future Fans (customers)

The first row is your current career. On the left is the "Personally invested artist you are." On the right is what you do: your blood, sweat and tears, your life's dream and passion: your life's work!

In between we find your current fans and success. Your current fans are your family and friends as well as fans who got to know you in "the early days." They love you and want to support you. But love is blind and I'm sorry to add it is often deaf, too. Plus, these people are ecstatic to imagine that someone they know – perhaps even a blood relative – is going to be a STAR!

When I say "current success" I mean the work, kudos and rewards of what you're experiencing now. The degree of success is immaterial. Your career has progressed since you started out, and wherever you are now is your current success.

Your current fans and success cannot be trusted. They are the cause of your floundering career. They are the reason why you're wrestling with the ideas in this book, and why you'll continue to make bad decisions about your career.

Consider one of my favorite book titles: "What Got You Here Won't Get You There," by Marshall Goldsmith. What it means is that you cannot base how you are doing and what you should do next based on current realities. You are simply too close and involved to make good decisions.

The solution? Become the CEO of You, Inc. as shown in row two.

CEO of You, Inc. is not a cute title. It is a mindset that will dramatically affect your life and career. The more you accept this title the more peace, joy, and success you will have. You must understand that you _are_ the CEO of You, Inc. whether you accept the title and responsibility or not.

By accepting the title of CEO of You, Inc. you move yourself to the center of the illustration. From that perspective, it is much easier to make right decisions. You can see the relationships between each of the components – yourself, your fans, your art and your prospective fans. Those relationships, viewed from the center, will help you determine your next steps.

So Mr. or Ms. CEO of You, Inc., let's start defining your product by talking about customers. Again.

Customers 102

Customers greatly complicate your life because they can do odd and unpredictable things. If you are basing your life on them – which you are – you will want to know what they're thinking.

You could ask them, but as you can see by Henry Ford's quote, they don't always know what they want. Plus, there are two more things to consider about customers: they don't buy products or services, and they have two reasons for their actions.

> If I had listened to customers I would've given them a faster horse.
>
> – Henry Ford

People don't buy products or services, people buy solutions to problems. A man does not buy a hammer; he buys a tool to put in a nail. A woman does not hire a lawn care company; she buys the perceived status of a beautifully kept home. No one buys art; they buy the emotions and thoughts that the art stirs inside of them.

I'll use cars to explain.

Why are there so many kinds of cars? Hasn't it occurred to anyone that they all do pretty much the same thing? Wouldn't one brand of two-door, four-door, pickup truck, and van be enough? Those four types would meet almost any need, right? Just think of how much easier car shopping would be, and we could get rid of all those car commercials that interrupt your favorite shows on TV!

That's not the way it is, though, is it? Instead, we see a non-stop parade of new cars offered every year. There are big ones, little ones, long ones, short ones, tall ones, low-riding ones, cheap ones, and ridiculously expensive ones.

Exactly WHY would anyone pay $200,000.00 for a Bentley when a $25,000.00 Kia does the exact same thing?

The problem with this kind of thinking is that it's focused on the product. To know why people buy a Bentley instead of a Kia, you must focus on the customer. It's not that you're wrong about both cars carrying people and their stuff. It's just that people want more than that from their automobiles. Let's look at what an owner of a Kia and Bentley get for their money:

Kia	Bentley
Transportation	Luxury
Function	Luxury
Inexpensive	Luxury
Nice style	Luxury
Gas mileage	Luxury
Great warranty	Luxury
------	Luxury
------	Luxury
------	Luxury

As we can see, the Kia buyer has satisfied a number of needs and desires that are all together different than the Bentley owner. Simple, right? Not really, because the buying decisions could go much deeper than function vs. luxury.

For instance, consider price. Let's say the Bentley costs eight times more than the Kia. So spending the $200,000 is a waste, right? Well, the argument could be made that the Bentley will run at least six to eight times longer than the Kia, and during those 40 to 50 years of use, the value of the Bentley will probably go up.

Suddenly, the Bentley's a STEAL! So why would anyone NOT buy a car packed with luxury that lasts 50 years and is worth more when you're done with it than when it's new? One reason might be a fundamental opposition to excessive purchases of any kind. The Bentley is definitely an excessive car with excessive leather trim and excessively bad gas mileage.

You'd be correct to point out that most people don't buy a Bentley for lack of $200 grand. Keep this in mind when thinking about your career and your product. People will only ultimately do what they can and nothing more. It doesn't matter if you are the most incredible artist since art began, people will not spend more than they can. No amount of incredible salesmanship is going to put a person with a Kia budget into a Bentley. Period.

Which brings us back to customers having two reasons for their actions. Ask any Kia-driving Bentley-lover why they bought their car and they're likely to say: "It's inexpensive and it gets great gas mileage!" But, the real reason is probably that they didn't have enough money to buy their dream car.

Consumers always have two reasons for doing what they do: The reason they tell you, and the REAL reason. (You'd do well to remember that this is true of people in most of life's situations. You can apply this to your relationships, work, hobbies, etc. This will explain many situations you will encounter.)

I'm not saying everyone is a liar (although, if the shoe fits...). I am saying there are two reasons for most people's actions, and sometimes even they don't know the real one. The man buying the hammer will say he's putting in a nail, but he may also want the hammer that will most impress his buddies. The woman wanting a nice lawn may also want to recreate something she remembers faintly from her childhood. The same could be said for their art related purchases, too. Art can bring people back to a time of special memories of days gone by.

So, how do you succeed despite your customers' spoken and unspoken problem-based needs? Combinations. Remember, the difference between failure and success in the arts and the real world will always come down to combinations of hard skills and soft skills - and of the two, soft skills are the most important.

The same things that are true about achieving personal success apply to product strategy. What separates a Kia from a Bentley is their unique combination of car and non-car attributes. Being cars is a given. Of course they're cars, and as we discussed, any car will get you and your stuff from here to there. In the end, what separates these two brands is their non-car attributes.

In the world of products, these "non" attributes are called value-adds. Consider the brands you love and you'll see what I mean. Starbucks sells coffee, Olive Garden serves food, Best Buy sells electronics and an iPod is a music player. Those statements are true, but there's so much more to say, right? Everything beyond the coffee, food, electronics and music player is a value-add.

And Mr. or Ms. CEO of You, Inc.: your value-add is *you*.

You, Inc. has Two Products

Earlier in this chapter I wrote about the "personally invested artist you are" as if it was a bad thing. That's because in the context of making decisions about your life and career, it is a bad thing. But in the context of your product, it is a good thing. In fact, it is THE thing.

The personally invested artist you are is what makes you unique. It is technically your value-add. But, you are far too important to be thought of as merely a "value-add." That's why I say You, Inc. has two products. Product #1 is your craft. Product #2 is literally *you,* and *you* cannot be duplicated by anyone in the world.

> Don't ask yourself what the world needs. Ask yourself what makes you come alive and go do that. Because what the world needs is people who have come alive.
>
> - Gil Bailie

If "What the world needs is people who have come alive," as Gil Bailie suggests, you must first make sure you're alive, and then connect with your customers at that level. We'll discuss your "aliveness" later.

For now, understand that your success is directly tied to your ability to express the personally invested artist you are. This is challenging because there's a fine line between just enough and too much. If you accept your role as CEO and consider both Product #1 and Product #2, you'll be better able to find that line.

Is It Soap Yet?

It is crucial to have the right perspective, and nothing gives better perspective about managing your career than thinking like a business owner. It allows you to consider all aspects of what you're doing when making decisions. In light of all you've learned as CEO of You, Inc., I ask you:
- Do you know what you do?
- What does your product sound, look and/or feel like?

- How do you describe what you do?
- What are the results from your playing, writing, acting, creating or performing?
- What are your customers getting in return for their money when they hire you to play, write, act, create or perform?
- Are they getting you?
- Are you connecting with customers in a way that matters to them?
- Do they know that you are personally invested in all that you do? If so, how do they know?
- If they don't know, what are you going to do about it?

Yes, there's a lot to figure out, but that's why CEOs get the big bucks! Speaking of big bucks, we need to figure out how to turn your soap into money, so you can eat. We need to create a marketing strategy and sales team. We need to talk about capital, which is just a fancy business term for money. But before we do, we're going to talk about you.

This should be fun.

CHAPTER 5

MY ATTITUDE

FAILED

As I scanned the row upon row of business cards on the bulletin board, it struck me how many drummers there were in Nashville.

Of the roughly 50 cards I saw, every third one was a drummer: steel player, guitarist, drummer. Guitar player, drummer, singer. Drummer, keyboardist, drummer.

I stood in the hallway of a rehearsal facility during a break. I was there as part of a band preparing for the first tour of the newly signed singer/songwriter and amazing guitarist, Anita Cochran. As I realized the odds against me I thought, "At least I'm making a living as a drummer."

When I was a musician, my life plan was to earn a living as a drummer. I wanted to provide for myself and my family by doing the thing I loved doing; the thing I had done since I was a child; the thing everyone told me I should do.

And that's what I did: I made a living as a drummer - and that was the problem.

It was a problem for two reasons: first, "making a living as a drummer" is a terrible goal. What exactly is "a living?" Is it defined by a certain income, house, food to eat, happiness? And what exactly did I want to *do*

> ## Decisions have descendants.
> ## What we choose today,
> ## we live tomorrow.
> ### - Kimberly Stephens

as a drummer? Did making a living as a drummer mean playing, teaching, writing? Did I want to play rock, jazz, country? With whom did I want to play? Did I want to tour, record, play clubs, play in a subway?

Without a clear answer to any of those questions (or maybe my answer to them all was, "YES!") the guiding principle of my life became work. If work was available, I took it. I used to joke that if the phone rang, I answered, "Yes, I'll do it. What is it?"

Funny, right? No. It was sad.

This life plan was also a problem because it was a lie. I didn't just want to make a living as a drummer, I wanted to be hog-nasty rich and travel the world. I wanted to play on projects with the best artists in the world and be known as one of the best recording and live drummers of our time. I wanted to own exotic sports cars and have homes in different countries. I wanted it all!

When I left the music business in 2001, it was *not* because I had succeeded at making a living by playing drums and wanted to try something else. I left the music business because I had failed to reach my ultimate goals; ultimate goals that I knew deep inside but never expressed to myself or others; ultimate goals that I hoped would come true.

It took leaving the music business for me to realize I got exactly the career I planned for. I made a living as a drummer – nothing less, but nothing more. Whether intentional or not, the plans we have direct our lives.

I failed in the creative arts because of my attitude.

The power of belief

Imagine the following scene in the boardroom of a Fortune 500 company:

"As you know, ladies and gentleman," says the Chairman of the Board, "today is the day we reorganize all the positions within our company. I have arranged for the names of each of our 543 employees to be written on individual slips of paper and placed inside our Staffing Barrel.

"In a moment, Thomas Blackmon, current VP of Business Affairs will read the titles of every job in our company. Susan Smith, our Senior VP of Human Resources will then rotate the barrel, open the small door, pull out a slip of paper and read the name. Her assistant Jim will record that person's new job title and we'll repeat the process until each job is filled. Shall we begin?"

Mr. Blackmon then says, "Vice President of Production" and nods to Susan.

As instructed, Susan spins the barrel, picks a slip and says "Overnight Mail Clerk, Andrew Johnston." Jim quickly finds Andrew Johnston on his list and replaces the words Overnight Mail Clerk with Vice President of Production. He asks Mr. Blackmon to read the next job title and can't help but smile about Andrew's good luck!

Can you imagine if this was the way Senior Executives at companies promoted and demoted people? Can you imagine anyone believing that's the way it's done? Neither can I.

Yet it is all too common to find people believing in luck.

Lies and Myths

A lie is a known untruth, especially with the intention to deceive. In my mind, I categorize luck as a lie. I've never seen any factual or personal basis for luck, and I think those that believe in luck are deceived in several ways.

People are deceived into missing the truth about what leads to success. Their belief in luck keeps them from seeing there is only one thing that leads to success of any kind: work. Thomas Edison once said, "Opportunity is missed by most people because it is dressed in overalls and looks like work."

In his 2008 book, *Outliers*, Malcolm Gladwell discussed numerous studies and his own research that show a minimum of 10,000 hours is needed to become "an expert" at anything. He points out that Mozart, Bill Gates, Steve Jobs and The Beatles all put in roughly 10,000 hours of practice before achieving their "overnight success."

It's not hard to find proof of hard work and dedication behind success, but those who believe in luck never look for it. This robs them of motivating and educating information that would help them reach their goals.

People who believe in luck think in terms of being outside of the lucky group. This Us vs. Them mindset blinds them to opportunities and options available for everyone. Rather than see the world as rich with possibilities, they see those possibilities as rich for everyone else. They can read the same articles as others and arrive at different conclusions.

Those that believe in luck see failure as final. In their minds, failure proves what they've known all along: that luck is for everyone but them, so they give up.

Did you know that Michael Jordan was cut from the basketball team as a sophomore in high school? How did he react? "I went to my room and I closed the door and cried, even though there was no one else home at the time, I kept the door shut. It was important to me that no one else hear me or see me."

Seeing that you're reading my book entitled, *Why I Failed in the Creative Arts and How NOT to Follow in My Footsteps,* it should come as no surprise that I'm especially passionate about this particular deception.

I'm passionate about this deception because it ruins lives. Nothing frustrates me more than people who have accepted failure as a given. They won't dream, won't hope, and in extreme but common cases, won't even work.

Oh, they have jobs, but they aren't working for anything but a paycheck. They say things like "Oh, I'm okay," or "I'm content with what I have," but their eyes give them away. They're not content at all.

They have within them a dream, idea, or solution that they stopped pursuing after a failure. They think about it often, resigned to the fact that it'll never be reality. They tried it. It failed.

No one should live that way. People are meant for far more than paychecks and hollow eyes. That's why they have their dreams, ideas, or solutions. They are meant to pursue them wholeheartedly and they are meant to fail.

Yes, you read that right: they are meant to fail. Failure is a crucial part of success.

Watch a baby learn to walk and you'll see. What seems like an endless string of bumbled attempts is actually a deep and rich learning experience for the baby. Every time they fail, they are getting thousands and thousands of pieces of data from the world around them (and a few bruises, too!). Each piece recalibrates their brains, nerves, and muscles for the next attempt.

Eventually, there's enough feedback about what NOT to do that the brain, nerves, and muscles walk the baby across the room. The baby has succeeded at walking because of the endless string of bumbled attempts otherwise known as failures.

Now, is it possible that somewhere there's a baby whose brain, nerves, and muscles get the necessary coordination together on the first attempt and walk the baby across the room? Yes, it's possible. It might have even happened.

But I ask you: would you like your child's ability to walk to be dependent on luck, or the tried and true failure method used by approximately 45,000 babies every day? If you can't decide, let me suggest that your "lucky" baby's second attempt to walk across the room will probably fail.

I can accept failure.

Everyone fails at something.

But I can't accept not trying.

— **Michael Jordan**

That's the problem with the other half of this topic: overnight success. Can you name one overnight success in the arts that has a career of any significant length of time? Before you answer, be sure to do the research I spoke of earlier. Almost anyone you believe to be an overnight success will be disqualified by at least 10,000 hours of hard work.

The rest of your names will fall into one of two categories: those that have continually improved and/or reinvented themselves, and those that...well...those that aren't on your list because they don't exist.

The rare, "true" overnight successes never last because they do not have the knowledge, experiences and relationships needed to maintain a long term career. They are like the baby who "lucked out" on the first try but doesn't have a clue how to do it again.

So, yes, I mean it when I say people are meant to fail. We are designed to learn by experiencing failure, recalibrating, and making another attempt. Each attempt grows us and strengthens us for long term success.

Three examples:
- Babe Ruth set a record for the most homeruns in a career (714) that stood from his retirement in 1935 until 1974. But he was also the strikeout king. He is still in the top 100 players with the most strikeouts with 1,330. Can you imagine anything more humiliating than taking the long walk back to the dugout from home plate 1,330 times?
- Thomas Edison tried over 10,000 designs of the light bulb before he found the design that has remained virtually unchanged ever since. No wonder he made the quote about work showing up in overalls. He lived it for years. Here's another Edison quote: "I haven't failed, I've found 10,000 ways that don't work."
- Once Michael Jordan finished crying, he went to work. He became the star of his school's junior varsity squad, and tallied several 40 point games by developing unmatched practice habits. Throughout his career, coaches called him the best practice player ever.

Jordan's long time coach Phil Jackson said: "The thing about Michael is, he takes nothing for granted. When he first came into the league in 1984, he was primarily a penetrator. His outside shooting wasn't up to professional standards. So he put in his gym time in the off-season, shooting hundreds of shots each day. Eventually, he became a deadly three-point shooter."

Success or Failure

I know and respect the fact that everyone has a different definition of success. No two people have the same dreams and goals, and that's how it should be. We will spend time defining dreams, goals and success later on, but for now, let's just agree that everyone wants to succeed and no one wants to fail.

All people, whether consciously or unconsciously, set out to reach their goals with the hope that they'll succeed. Furthermore, 100% of people either succeed or fail to reach those goals.

My intent in this chapter is to discuss the reason some people fail and quit, while others fail and succeed. The reason is simply this: successful people think and act differently than un-successful people.

Yes, it sounds simplistic, obvious, and empty, but consider the statement carefully. *Successful people think and act differently than un-successful people.* It may, indeed, be simplistic, but it is anything but empty. In fact, it may be the most jam-packed statement in this book.

Successful people and non-successful people spend their lives thinking and acting. Both successful and un-successful people will end up in life exactly where their thoughts and actions lead them. The difference is successful people succeed by choosing successful thoughts and actions.

Now, let me say I am fully aware that there are circumstances that prevent people from achieving their goals. Life is not always fair, and trials and tribulations will come along. Some tribulations will be small and some may be insurmountable. But even in cases of insurmountable odds, you'll see that success, true success, is found in the attitudes and actions of the people who find it, despite the hardships and challenges that life throws their way.

Attitude and Actions

I drove home from work one evening last winter. My route was mostly interstate highway, but the last portion of the commute was a narrow and winding road without a shoulder of any kind. At an intersection a few streets from my house, some jerk pulled in front of me and cut me off.

I couldn't believe I had to slow down like that! Jeez, the nerve of that guy!

So of course, I sped up and ran him right off the road and out of the way. Served him right too, he made me mad and I had to get even with him!

> You cannot control what happens to you, but you can control your attitude toward what happens to you, and in that, you will be mastering change rather than allowing it to master you.
>
> - Brian Tracy

That's not what really happened, but it could've been. I could've pushed his car into the ditch. I was mad and I would've been justified too, right?

Well, no, and here's why: this driver did not make me mad, I did, one step at a time.

I interpreted his driving as a personal challenge to my path home, which is silly. It's highly unlikely that he spent the afternoon at home scheming to pull in front of me at 6:15 that Tuesday evening.

I selected anger from a multitude of responses. I could have chosen thankfulness that I wasn't hit, concern about his sobriety (or lack of brains), a petition to have the road widened, or nothing more than a "Whoa!" I chose to get mad.

The driver's involvement stopped at the moment he drove his car in front of mine. Everything else happened in my brain and only in my brain. He did not give me disgust, anger, and the desire for revenge, I found them myself.

Attitude is a little thing that makes a big difference.

— Winston Churchill

They were my disgust, my anger, and my desire for revenge. Had I chosen to follow them to the next logical conclusion, they would have resulted in my action of running the guy off the road.

As Brian Tracy's quote suggests, I did not have control over the other driver, but I did have control over my attitude towards him and what he did. I had control over whether I would master the situation or whether it would master me.

Thankfully, I chose to control myself and drove home to a nice warm dinner (sure beats prison food).

Before we move on, and before you rip my eyes out, control your thoughts and actions and allow me to make an important disclaimer: I know there are extreme, violent, and life threatening circumstances where another human can control your actions. These circumstances are beyond the realm of this discussion and if you have experienced such circumstances, I strongly suggest the counsel and guidance of a trained professional.

This discussion is about our choices in day-to-day life. The choices everyone makes to take control of their own thoughts and actions, or to live as victims of the "They made me do it," "Life's not fair," and "I'm owed this" mindset that runs rampant in our society.

One of the greatest insights into this topic comes from Viktor Frankl, a World War II concentration camp prisoner. Like most victims of those camps, he was a firsthand witness to some of the most violent and sadistic behaviors in human history. Time after time, he saw friends, family members, and fellow prisoners die from starvation, torture, or gas chambers.

Viktor Frankl lived through this ordeal and went on to become a major proponent of what we're discussing here. During his time in Auschwitz, he saw how character traits affected his fellow prisoners.

Because of his observations, he decided that despite his tragic and frightening surroundings, and the fact that they had taken away everything he had externally, he would not let them control his mind. He kept his mind focused on a worthwhile goal – walking out alive – and he not only achieved it, he also walked out free of many of the mental scars that continually haunt other survivors.

His choices controlled his thoughts under tremendous duress. In turn he was able to control some of his actions by ultimately walking to freedom. Viktor Frankl was a successful person. Not only did he survive, he survived with the greatest treasure he had – himself.

If you are to succeed in your life, you must possess the same mental capacity. Why? Because your life will be full of challenges and circumstances you can't control, and though they cannot remotely compare to a concentration camp, they are challenges that must be overcome. Overcoming is an action, and actions come from attitude.

Response-Ability

You have a responsibility to live this way. You literally have the ability to respond to what happens in your life. How you choose to respond will lead to failure or success.

This explains why two people from the same circumstances can end up in such different places. How many thousands of kids other than Michael Jordan experienced the same loss of being cut from their High School basketball team? Some chose to quit. Jordan responded by working harder. His thoughts led to actions that led to success.

Understand the order of these events: Thoughts and actions precede success, not the other way around. You have to think like a success, then work like a success, before you can be a success. As Robert Kiyosaki says: "be-do-have."

Willing to Change

Wanting stuff and a better life is easy. Everyone wishes and hopes for the things they desire. Some people respond to their wishes and hopes, change their attitudes and act.

> You must be the change you wish to see in the world.
>
> — Mahatma Gandhi

I hope that's what you'll do.

Before I leave this subject however, I must give you a warning that sooner or later you will hit a wall. It will be a solid barrier between you and your success and it will be one that you made yourself.

It will be a wall built by desires, thoughts, ideals, beliefs, habits, boredom, or at worst, addictions. You will have a choice to make: a fundamental, deeper than responsive attitude choice. It will be a choice between things that you love.

A mentor of mine, the late Dr. Barry Grove, used to say, "A fantasy is something you think you can have without changing." In other words, whatever you think you can have without changing is a fantasy.

The change may take many forms. Working out each morning may require you go to bed early the night before. Saving for a new car may keep you from eating out as often as you'd like. Pursuing a career in the arts means honing your craft while your friends are having fun, networking when you'd rather be home, doing without because you're out of money, and living in a city with your chosen industry so you can find work.

The way to manage these choices will be prioritization. You'll have to pick the things you love over things you love less. Some of your choices will be temporary as you set aside something for a season. Others will be permanent.

Which brings me to the last quote of this chapter:

> Not everything that is faced can be changed, but nothing can be changed until it is faced.
>
> — James Baldwin

The core message of this chapter is change - changed responsibility, attitude, actions and priorities. We discussed your ability to respond to the world around you, how changing your attitude can change your actions, and how changed actions affect your life.

You will be unable to make any of these changes if you are not honest with yourself, so put on your CEO hat whenever possible. You will be better able to face the realities of your life and make better decisions.
It will also help you face the realities of your career. After all, the only thing worse than failure is succeeding at the wrong thing.

CHAPTER 6

I WAS DREAMING

Sometime in the early 80's I read an interview with Jeff Porcaro, the legendary late drummer for Toto.

I idolized Jeff for his playing and his career. What little plan I had for my career was based on his: I was going to be just like Jeff.

I was going to play drums in a famous band. Yes, I wanted to be famous, but what I wanted more was creative freedom. I wanted to contribute my ideas and style to the creation of music and help make the band famous.

Then I wanted to use the fame to get work as a session drummer and side man with other artists specifically because they wanted my ideas and style. In my mind, everything I just said described the career of Jeff Porcaro.

Then I read the interview.

About halfway through it, he talked about the misconceptions he and many other people have about the recording industry. Instead of the endless hours of creative music making, he said he often found himself adding last minute parts to almost finished songs.

Jeff spoke of one particular session where he was asked to add a boring, hi-hat part to a song. The song was lousy and the part didn't fit, but that's what he was hired to do, so he sat alone in the studio, played the part, and went home.

That interview was my first clue that I knew very little about the music industry. It was a clue that my life's dream might not be based on reality. It was a clue that should have led me to look for more clues.

I blew it off by thinking, "He must be doing it wrong."

This pattern of denying reality continued for years as I did work I didn't want to do either. It hid the fact that I was not happy with big chunks of my life and that I should have made changes - changes that would have helped me build a long term career.

I failed in the creative arts because I was dreaming.

Is what you want real? Make sure

Disillusioned

Among his many talents, my son is an amazing actor. Most of his experience so far has been on the stage since he's only done a small amount of film and video work.

Last weekend he participated in a film project competition here in Middle Tennessee. He left the house at 7:30 and didn't get home until well after midnight.

When I asked him the next day how it had gone, he said he had learned a lot from amazing conversations, met some great people, had spent too much money on food and been on camera 5 seconds.

5 seconds.

Though his experience is a bit extreme, it's not at all unusual. My own experience with filming music videos supports the fact that there's way more prep time than actual filming.

I'm glad he's had that experience *before* he decides to make a living in movies. It will help make the right decision about his chosen industry before he makes the leap. Realities are always a good thing to know.

Careers, Fields, and Jobs

As you learn about your industry, it will help to know the difference between a job, a field, and a career. Though people mix them up, they have different meanings and different ways they fit together. Making sense of the differences will help you as you put together your plan.

FreeDictionary.com defines *Job* as a "Regular activity performed in exchange for payment." This "activity" can be done part time or full time. It can be done once, or over and over again, and the payment is usually money (an exchange). Acting is a job; so is writing scripts.

Most dictionary definitions of the word *Field* are so long and confusing that I can't make any sense of them at all. I say a field is a grouping of similar skills, jobs, or interests - sometimes all three. Visual Art is a field. It is a group of skills like understanding technique, materials and perspective. It is also a group of jobs: painting, sculpting, etc.

The Oxford English Dictionary defines *Career* as "An individual's course or progress through life or a distinct portion of life." The "course or progress" is made up of groups of jobs and/or fields. I had a 20 year career as a musician, then I became a businessman.

I could've chosen a different path and had a career as a businessman, in the field of music, working as a concert promoter. Or a teacher, in the field of adult education, making drum lesson videos. Or a teacher, in music, writing books like *Why I Failed in the Creative Arts*.

As you research your industry, think about what you want to do in terms of job, field, and career. It's not enough that you call yourself by what you do (actor, photographer, dancer, etc.). Is that your career or your job? It's also not enough to say you're going to make a living in dance. That's too broad. Do you mean modern of classical? Live performance or film? On stage or choreography?

This is not about locking down your life for a plan you can never change. It's about helping you put the things you learn about the industry into the right place in your plan; a plan that will then be useful and meaningful.

It is also about making sure you can tell other people what you do, so they think of you when they want what you do; which is called marketing.

You, Inc. Needs a Marketing Plan

Marketing and the related activity, Sales, are misunderstood terms. Most people think they mean less than they do, and they see them as separate things. Still others shudder at the mention of the words because of visions of bad television commercials for used cars.

Consider this: if you've ever discussed your opinions with someone, you have marketed. If you've ever captured the attention of a someone special, you have marketed. If you've ever gotten a date with that someone special, you've marketed and sold. If you married that someone special, you're a professional!

Don't be put off by the terms marketing and sales. Understanding what they are and how to do them is easy. Putting them into practice will be well worth your efforts.

Marketing 101

My simple rules of Marketing (and Sales):
1. Marketing is more than a message.
2. Marketing is about the customer.
3. You are never *not* marketing
4. If you market correctly, sales will happen.

Rule 1 - Marketing is more than a message.

> "I'm Lovin' It" - McDonald's
> "Like a Good Neighbor" - State Farm
> "They're Grrrrr-REAT!" - Frosted Flakes
> "Live to Ride" - Harley Davidson

Slogans like these are a small, but highly noticeable part of marketing, but they are not the only part. There is so much more:

- Early research - Who is the customer, what do they want, and where are they?
- Product/service design - How will the product/service meet the needs and/or wants of those customers?
- Packaging - How will the product/service attract those customers?
- Sales design - Where do those customers shop?
- Pricing - How much can the customer pay, and how much _will_ they pay?
- Advertising - How will you tell the customer about the product or service in a way that they'll "get it?"
- Research - Is the customer happy?

This is actually a list of everything discussed in this book. We've talked about each of these steps as they relate to you, your art, your fans, and how you'll make a living. We've used different terms in some cases, but we've covered them all. They are all Marketing.

Rule 2 - Marketing is about the customer.

In fact, your entire career is about the customer- that is, if you want to make a living.

Now, I am NOT saying you have to sell out. The only reason people sell out is because they have never figured out _who_ likes what they're doing and _how_ to reach those people.

You'll never have to sell out if you take the time to think about your customers first, and always. Believe me, in this wide world there are customers who want your art, and they want you to find them.

If you don't, two things will happen. First, you will spend your life trying to connect with the wrong people - which won't work so you'll end up frustrated. Second, you will miss out on making the right connection with the right people - in which case you'll also end up frustrated.

I assume you understand why you'll be frustrated. What you may not understand is why the right people will be frustrated, too.

Rule 3 - You are never *not* marketing.

The right people will be frustrated because they won't be able to like you, even if they love your art. Why? Because everything you do and say will be telling them they don't matter. They will clearly understand that even though the art is what they want, the artist doesn't "get them."

Remember, you are never *not* marketing. You simply do not have that choice. You cannot decide that you don't want to market, or that you only want to market part of the time. Even if you do decide to not market, you will still be marketing. You'll just be doing it badly.
And your customers will know it.

My 1st simple rule says marketing is more than a message, and that's true. What is also true is that the focus of marketing is the touch point between a product/service and the customer. Every touch point is about communication. In this way, marketing is in fact, a message. It is the message that everyone sees and hears every time there's a touch. Which is why those bad used car commercials rarely work.

Rule 4 - If you market correctly, sales will happen.

Put all this together and you have a product/service that connects with a customer on a personal level.
- It meets their need or want.
- It's found where they expect it and want it.
- It's attractive in appearance/features and price.
- They learn about it in a way that makes sense.

The end result is a sale.

When marketing is done well, sales happen, and they happen simply, easily, and without much effort.

Marketing 102

There are many, many books written on marketing. You'll find some of the information contained in some of those books to be helpful if you want to learn more about marketing.

Let me warn you right up front that many of those many, many books are junk - especially the ones that talk about getting rich quick. Let me give you two ideas and a tool that you'll find in some of those books. It'll get you started and also help you decide if you'd like to learn more.

The first idea is The 4 P's of marketing: Product, Place, Price, and Promotion. These four words are the "buckets" used by professional marketers.

- Product - the design and function of the product/service itself along with it's packaging
- Place - where the product/service fits in the market. This covers decisions like whether it's a value or high end product/service, or where will it be sold.
- Price - obviously, the cost to purchase.
- Promotion - what will be said about the product/service in ads and offers.

If the product, place, price, and promotion are right, sales will happen.

Next, is a tool called The SWOT Analysis. It can get as complicated as it sounds and it also has a fancy diagram that can be used, too. All you need to know is what it is and how it works.

SWOT is an acronym for Strengths, Weaknesses, Opportunities, and Threats. The simplest way to use this tool is to divide a sheet of paper into four parts by drawing a line down the center and another across the middle. Then write each of the words in its own section like this:

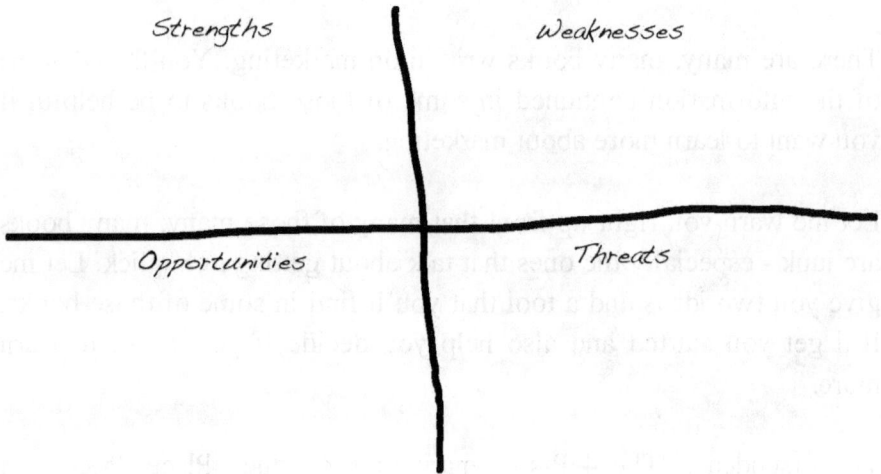

Strengths	Weaknesses
Opportunities	Threats

Once you have a drawing like that, answer these questions about yourself and your world:

- Strengths: what are the things I do well?
- Weaknesses: what are the things I should or could do well, but I don't?
- Opportunities: what are the jobs, gigs and/or ideas I could do that are real today (in other words, this isn't the place for fantasies - write down real opportunities that are available)?
- Threats: what are the things that could limit or take away those opportunities, or the people who could get that work?

A couple of things to note: The top boxes are about you. Your answers are about your strengths and your weaknesses. The bottom boxes are about things and/or people outside of you.

Examples of opportunities are things like: Move to L.A., live with cousin. Take local gig, use money for lessons. Examples of threats are things like: High rent keeps me from buying a new camera. Jim wants my current role and he's better than I am. The threats box is not for things like Global Warming or Terrorism unless these are directly affecting your work.

I like the SWOT tool for two reasons.

First, there's something about getting information like this onto a sheet of paper. Not only does it get it out of your head, but seeing it helps you make more sense of what you're thinking.

Second, it helps you spot connections that can lead to solutions. For instance, what strengths do you have that you can use to get an opportunity? Is there a strength that helps deal with a threat? What about your weaknesses? What can you do about the ones that matter?

The last idea is the Life Cycle Diagram, sometimes called the Bell Curve because of its shape. Here's the diagram:

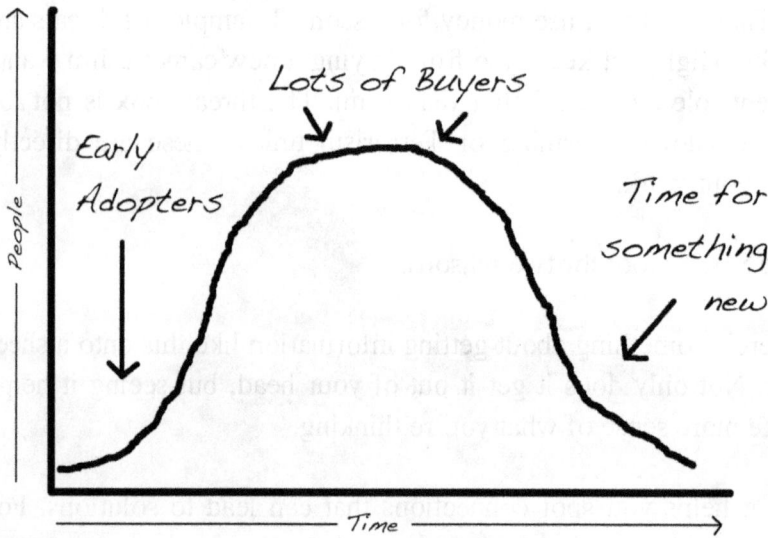

The diagram shows how the normal lifecycle of products/services at it starts, grows, levels off, and then dies out.

Left to right, the bottom shows time from when a product is introduced to when no one wants to buy it anymore. From bottom to top, the left side shows how many people buy the product.

The curve shows that when a product is new, no one buys it. Soon, however, a few daring people buy the product. These people, officially called "Early Adopters" love the product and tell all their friends. Soon, more people buy it and the curve goes up.

Eventually, the number of people buying the product levels off. This could be because it's not popular or there simply aren't any customers left to buy it (this is called saturation - just like a sponge can only hold so much water, a market can only buy so much of a product).

Once the leveling off point is reached, it's only a matter of time before the sales slow and eventually stop. The lifecycle for that product is done.

Two thoughts:

1. My career followed this same path and so will yours. I suggest you figure out where you are on the curve today and how to keep yourself on the left part or in the center for as long as possible. It can be done, and my second thought tells you how.

2. Always be thinking of ways to put yourself and/or your art on the left side of the diagram while also keeping the center alive and well. In other words, make new art, work with someone new and unexpected. Experiment. Create. You know what I mean: be creative!

There are many other tools used in the marketing process. Whether you choose to use these or others is not as important as whether or not you continue to think like a CEO. CEOs understand the importance of knowing not only what their company does, but how it fits with other companies in the marketplace, and how it meets the needs of customers.

> Failures don't plan to fail; they fail to plan.
>
> — Harvey Mackay

Once CEOs begin to have a grasp of that knowledge, they realize the importance of having a plan.

CHAPTER 7

I Was Hoping

In 1995, I got a call to sub on a recording session when the original drummer pulled out at the last minute.

It was a call to play for a new publishing company and I was excited about the opportunity to work with new writers and the music veteran that owned the company. At the time I was struggling to rebuild my career after the Gibson/Miller Band fell apart the year before. I desperately needed the work and the call was a much needed opportunity.

Every artist has experienced moments when everything works right - this was one of those days. The songs were great, the musicians were top notch, and I was inspired to play a number of ideas that blew everyone away.

Compliments flew my way all day long as every writer said I made their songs come alive beyond their dreams. By the end of the day I was passing out business cards like candy. The owner of the company loved what I did and I left there certain they would call me again, soon and often.

I never heard from them again.

Besides not having the work, the most frustrating part was that I had no idea why they never called. Not only had I done what they needed, but I had done it better than it had been done before! They TOLD me so. Why didn't they call?

I had such high hopes!

This story is a perfect example of how I pursued my career as a drummer. First, a call came out of nowhere and I got a gig. Next, I played great. Then, I sat around hoping another call would come.

It never dawned on me that they might need reminders about who I was, what I had done, and why they needed it again. It never dawned on me to follow-up in anyway at all.

It never dawned on me because I only had one thing on my mind: playing drums well.

I failed in the creative arts because I was hoping.

The power of a right goal

From Tom Watson, founder of IBM:

"IBM is what it is today for three special reasons. The first reason is that, at the very beginning, I had a very clear picture of what the company would look like when it was finally done. You might say I had a model in my mind of what it would look like when the dream – my vision – was in place.

"The second reason was that once I had that picture, I then asked myself how a company which looked like that would have to act. I then created a picture of how IBM would act when it was finally done.

"The third reason IBM has been so successful was that once I had a picture of how IBM would look like when the dream was in place and how such a company would have to act, I then realized that, unless we began to act that way from the very beginning, we would never get there.

"In other words, I realized that for IBM to become a great company it would have to act like a great company long before it ever became one.

"From the very outset, IBM was fashioned after the template of my vision. And each and every day we attempted to model the company after that template. At the end of each day, we asked ourselves how well we did, and discovered the disparity between where we were and where we had committed ourselves to be, and, at the start of the following day, set out to make up for the difference.

"Every day at IBM was a day devoted to business development, not doing business. We didn't *do* business at IBM, we *built* one."

$1,440

Congratulations, from this day forward, you will receive $1,440 each morning for the rest of your life. The catch? You must spend or invest every dollar by the end of each day. Any money left over is immediately worthless at the stroke of midnight.

If that happened, I'd guess you would immediately write a list of all the things you wanted to buy - and you'd discover that it's actually a tricky list to write. The fact that the money expires each night means you can't buy houses, cars or other big ticket items. You could

> The future is something which everyone reaches at the rate of sixty minutes an hour, whatever he does, whoever he is.
>
> - C. S. Lewis

come up with plenty of ways to spend the $1,440 each day, but eventually you'd run out of things to buy. What then?

After days, weeks, or months of watching $1,440 expire each night, a mental shift would occur and you would begin to invest. You'd invest in opportunities that earned you more money so you could buy the house and the car.

Spending, wasting, and investing money are familiar concepts. We understand these concepts because money is a valuable resource. If we are wise, we establish budgets and plans to carefully and responsibly manage the money we earn for now and the future.

But what about time? Might the same principles also apply to time? It should. Don't you consider time to be a valuable resource, too?

1,440 Minutes

We begin each day with 1,440 minutes that are ours to use as we wish. We can spend them: "I'm going to spend today with my family at the beach." We can waste them: "Wow, that movie stole two hours of my life that I'll never get back!" Or, we can invest them: "We've got to invest in this relationship if we are going to stay together."

It's important to note that, unlike money, investing time does not yield more time. Nothing yields more time. We're given 1,440 minutes to spend each day and at the stroke of midnight, they're gone.

Everyone has time. It is given freely to people of all races, religions, colors, nationalities, beliefs, and creeds. Time is the ultimate example of equal opportunity, and that is its power. Time makes presidents of some and criminals of others. It builds marriages, bridges, cities, and countries - and can destroy them all in an instant.

> By labor we can find food and water, but all of our labor will not find for us another hour.
>
> - Kenneth Patton

At least, that's what many believe.

But time doesn't do any of those things. Time is in fact, powerless. What is time exactly? It is a word we use all the...well, time. But what is it, really?

Time is nature's way of keeping everything from happening at once. Or as the Oxford English Dictionary more formally defines it, time is "The indefinite continued progress of existence and events in the past, present, and future, regarded as a whole." The American Heritage Dictionary says time is "A non-spatial linear continuum in which events occur in an apparently irreversible succession."

Call me weird, but "A non-spatial linear continuum in which events occur in an apparently irreversible succession," is my favorite. In simpler terms, it says time can't be seen, tasted, or felt, yet it's ongoing, all affecting, and irreversible.

As a wise man once observed, "Time stops for no man."

So what are you doing with the 1,440 minutes you received today? What will you do with the ones you'll get tomorrow? Think carefully before you answer. Your answers determine your life.

> Dost thou love life? Then do not squander time, for that's the stuff life is made of.
>
> - Benjamin Franklin

If you're going to live tomorrow what you choose today, you should know how you want to live tomorrow, right? Having a clear vision of the tomorrow you'd like to have will improve your chances of making the correct decisions today.

You have time. You need goals.

Gols (it's not a typo)

We are all familiar with the word, goal. From our earliest childhood we've understood the word to mean, target. We've also understood the importance of reaching a goal. It's therefore easy for us to grasp the fact that having a goal brings direction to the things we do and say.

But the root of the word goal suggests an additional benefit. The origin of our word goal is gol. Gol is an Old English word for the rows of rocks or small shrubs that separated farmers' fields. A more direct translation of the word gol would be boundary.

> How we spend our days is, of course, how we spend our lives.
>
> **- Annie Dillard**

The gols were the boundary that defined where the farmer would work and where he would not.

This background explains what I think is the most important, powerful part of goals: eliminating distractions. Why? Because having the right boundary between what you will do and what you will not do is HUGE!

Imagine a kid in a candy story. There's so much to choose from, he's going crazy! First he picks up gum drops, but then he sees the lollipops. "Got it!" he says, but spots the chocolate aisle out of the corner of his eye.

He'll either never choose for fear of choosing the wrong candy, or choose them all and have the mother of all belly aches to prove it later on.

A wise parent helps the child by limiting the choices. Whether by cost, aisle or kind, the parent says, "Here's what you can choose from and no more."

Fewer choices limit the confusion and help the child focus on making a choice. The kid doesn't have to worry about every piece of candy in the store; he picks from the few he can have and moves on.

Which brings me to the Number One reason I failed in the arts: I played too many gigs on the wrong side of my (unspoken and unwritten) boundary.

Instead of working as a creatively inspiring pop/rock drummer, I became a drummer that could and would play anything, anytime, anywhere, and for just about any price.

Note that I used the word *became* because I mean it, literally.

Over time, the cycle of play anything, anytime, anywhere, and for just about any price meant that I was that drummer. It no longer mattered what I wanted to be, or what I thought I was being. I was the "any drummer."

Wasted Days and Wasted Nights.

- Freddy Fender

The people who hired *any drummer* didn't have a particularly strong reason to hire me, so in order to make a living playing drums, I had to work for a LOT of people who hired *any drummer*. Which meant, of course, that I didn't have much time left to get the attention of the people who needed a creatively inspiring pop/rock drummer.

I worked myself out of having the career I wanted because I had created the perfect negative feedback loop.

A feedback loop is a description of events or reactions that feed similar events or reactions in a continuous loop. Feedback loops can be positive or negative depending on what's being fed back.

In my case the more "any drummer" work I took, the more of it I got, and the more I became any drummer.

Good goals would have focused my activities. Great goals would have inspired me to do those activities. Mine were somewhere between good and great as evidenced by the success I did achieve, but there's another level: right goals. In addition to inspiring my activities, right goals would have also kept me from pursuing all unrelated activities. That is the power of right goals.

Goals

Right goals are one of those things that are easy to define, but hard to create. With guidance and thought however, you can create right goals for yourself. Here are some things to keep in mind:

- **Write** – It's been proven that people who write down goals are more likely to achieve them than those that don't.
- **Gols** – Start with a list of things you can do to earn money. This gives you an initial list of real options – options that you could actually do and options that will continually create distractions too.
- **Specific** – Remove anything from your list that's not specific. If you struggle a bit with this, the next steps will help.
- **Measurable** – Remove or rewrite anything on your list that can't be measured. For example, as previously explained, making a living is not measurable, but making $75,000 per year is. Dancing for an international, 100-city tour is an example of a clearly measurable goal.
- **Attainable** – Considering that the first step of defining your gols gave us a list of things you can really do, the question of attainable is here to define an appropriate level of achievement for you. For instance, an extreme fear of flying would make the goal of dancing for that international, 100-city tour unattainable. On a more personal level, this is the step where you reflect deeply about your abilities and make sure your goals are, well…attainable.
- **Realistic** – While attainable is about you, realistic is defined by external factors. Making $75,000 a year as a photographer is realistic. Making $75 billion a year as a photographer is not, simply because of economics. This is the step where you rid your list of goals such as "Being the best in the world."

- **Time based** – When will you achieve each item on your list of specific, measurable, attainable, and realistic goals? I love this last step because time is the ultimate gol.
- **Displayed** – When your goal list is complete, post it where you'll see it. Often.

Congratulations, you are now the proud owner of a list of S.M.A.R.T. gols - Specific, Measurable, Attainable, Realistic and Time based boundaries and targets.

Unexpected Benefits

You now understand the fact that goals guide your activities by providing a focus on your desired outcome. You also have the added Old English perspective that goals, or gols, provide boundaries that keep distractions out of your way.

But wait, that's not all. There are two additional, and unexpected, benefits to having goals.

First, goals give you a fresh awareness of the world around you. Books and magazine articles you once ignored will now somehow seem relevant and useful. You'll find common ground and connections with people where none used to exist. All of these resources will become a tremendous boost to your progress.

Second, goals free up your life. Actually, gols free up your life. Just like the farmer reaching the gol at the end of his field and turning around, your goals will clearly show you when you've done enough. Knowing you've done enough means you can be free to stop working. Not working means you're free to actually spend time living, and that's what you really want, isn't it? Well, isn't it?

CHAPTER 8

I Wanted To Be A Star

I was pacing again.

I paced most mornings for the nearly two years I had wrestled and argued with God about the failure of my music career.

I still hadn't figured out what had happened, and I was torn between two fears: the fear of failing to rebuild my music career and the fear of not knowing how to support my family any other way.

I still had a strong desire to play drums. It was what I had done all my life, what I felt most comfortable doing, and what I loved. While pacing back and forth and thinking out loud, I said something about the fact that drumming had also been the way I had provided the comfortable and consistent lifestyle my family and I enjoyed.
My reaction caught me off guard - I hated that lifestyle.

Up until that moment, I had been blinded; blinded by my love for music, the fact that I was good, and my desires to be hog-nasty rich, travel the world, play on projects with the best artists in the world, be known as one of the best recording and live drummers of my time, own exotic sports cars, and have homes in different countries.

I had been blinded by a deep-seated, and society-fed desire to be a ROCK STAR! And that desire kept me blinded in two ways.

It kept me blinded to the reality that I hated our lifestyle. I hated the uncertain schedule and uncertain finances. I hated the constant search for work and the constant chasing to get paid. I hated the factory-work mentality and the rarity of creating art. I hated the time away from home and all the things I missed when I was gone. I had been blind to the reality that our lifestyle was neither comfortable, consistent, or enjoyed.

It also kept me blinded to my real desires; desires for enjoyable and creative work, enough money for a nice home and some nice things, but most importantly, a family and friends with which to enjoy all this.

I failed in the creative arts because I wanted to be a star.

What you want is a LIFE!

Professional goals are important, as I hope the first seven chapters of this book have taught you. But as you'll see, they are worthless if they do not support a clear set of personal goals. Personal goals about the life you want to live, where you want to live, and who you want to share it with.

Get a sheet of paper and write the numerals 1 - 20 down the left hand side of the page. In no particular order, write things you'd like to achieve, have, or do that don't involve work. Don't worry about time or money, this is simply a list of ideas, so think freely and let your imagination go wild.

If you're like most people, you'll be challenged by this assignment. You'll find it difficult to think of anything that doesn't involve work. Society has taught you to define yourself by your work, but nothing could be farther from the truth. The fact that this is difficult is exactly why it matters.

As a creative you'll feel justified in ignoring this rule, because your work is your art and your art is your work. I get that, but I don't care. Despite how you feel, this art/work thing is not unique to artists. Besides, it's also a lie. You - the person - are not defined by your output while on this planet, even if your output *is* art.

So, yes, I mean it when I tell you to make sure that nothing on the list involves work.

Without work and/or art, you'll be challenged because what's left is so...personal. Despite the fact that we're all selfish and self-centered by nature, something in us shuts down when asked about ourselves. Push through. There's nothing more important than uncovering the deep desires of your heart.

Once uncovered, you're next challenge will be defining them. Tangible, a+b=c, task-oriented things we'd like to do are easy to define, but when it comes to the life we'd like to live, we're fuzzy at best. How exactly do you define "time with friends?" It's one of those things that we all know but struggle to explain.

Explain it anyway. Keep in mind that this list, like all the professional items we listed earlier, is subject to change. The important thing to remember is that unwritten, vague, and fuzzy goals are never achieved. Never. Your personal goals *must* be achieved, so write them down in as much detail as you can.

Be sure your list has ongoing items, too, not just someday items. Just like the most successful diets allow for desserts in moderation, your personal goals must include things you will enjoy during your journey to your ultimate goals. All work and no play makes Jack a dull boy. It also makes him burnout and quit. Make sure your list includes a few desserts.

Stick-to-it-tiveness

Success that's worth achieving is not easy. If you expect anything less than hard work, pain, difficulty, struggle, failure, and occasional overwhelming confusion don't bother pursuing a career in the arts. In fact, don't bother pursuing a career in any business.

The pursuit of your professional and personal goals will be difficult. It will be challenged. Often. Strongly. Persistently. It will be challenged in direct proportion to the importance of your goals and your passion to reach them.

If you think I'm trying to discourage you...you're right. I'm discouraging you from settling on small, weak, and selfish goals that will never sustain you against the odds you'll face.

I'm encouraging you to have large goals that turn you on and fire you up. It's even better if they scare you just a bit. I'm encouraging you to have strong goals that you can see clearly enough to taste, see, and feel. I am encouraging you to have goals that are bigger than you.

Two Thoughts:
1. I'm not suggesting you have to save the planet from global warming or cure cancer, but chances are you do have a few goals that are bigger than yourself, such as a charity you want to support, people you want to reach with your message (beyond making them smile and/or dance), a family member or friend that you want to repay, or a cause you want to further.
2. Self-serving goals are weak motivators. Sooner or later, you'll reach a point where you'll say, "Why bother?" and without the pressure of others depending on your success, you'll quit.

Find something that you want to accomplish that's bigger than yourself and make it a part of your goals.

You

At the beginning of this book I ripped apart the myth of talent and its contribution to success. I did that to strip you of the one thing you've been most dependent on your whole life; a dependence that not only determined your attitude, dreams, hopes, and actions, but your opinion of yourself.

Then, I purposefully asked you to explore your thoughts, ideas, and desires from every angle. While this was done with your career in mind, my goal was both deeper and wider.

Eternity

We all have questions; questions about why we're here and "The meaning of it all," questions that we decide not to ask because they do not come from conscious thought or will. They are questions that are as much a part of our design as our need for water and oxygen. The questions are real and they must be asked, and the answers must be revealed.

They are part of The Story.

Think of the stories that have filled the books, songs, stages, and theaters of human history. Think of the tales told around campfires and around the world. There are universal themes found in them all; themes that are mythic in their nature, and mythic in their consistency; themes of wars between good and evil, average people living grand adventures and fighting unbeatable enemies, average people revealed as heroes in the end. And finally, love. There is always love.

Why do we like these stories? Why do we - all of us - identify with them? Why are these stories found in every nation, tribe, and tongue on earth? Perhaps we identify with them because they inspire us, yet I propose just the opposite. I propose that we are inspired because this story is a part of our identity.

Something about us agrees with this story; subconsciously, deeply, spiritually. We agree with the plot and the cast of characters. We relate to the average person and long to be the hero; to live an adventure, and defeat a terrible foe. To explore the world and change the course of history. To matter.

Which is why I suggested you establish a goal bigger than yourself. You need to be aware of the fact that you want to do more than simply to create your art. Like the hero in these stories, you want to live out your adventure, and win the battles you will face.

And you want to be loved.

There's always love.

The universal and unchanging theme of The Story is love. The universal and unchanging theme of *your* story is love. And unless you recognize and properly deal with this need, your life will become a series of vain attempts to fill your heart with gigs, applause, the trappings of success, and positive reviews.

This need for love will not go away and it cannot be ignored. It is like the questions I mentioned above. It is a part of your design. In fact, they are linked. You have the questions and the need because of the One who loves: the Creator of the Universe described in Genesis.

I write this for two reasons:

First, there is simply too much spiritual and physical evidence to dismiss the existence of God. In addition to the universal questions, themes, and needs I've discussed here, scientists are increasingly arriving at the conclusion that there's more to our universe than they can explain. Do the research and you'll find them either completely stumped or supportive of the Creator - often disguised as "intelligent design."

Second, experience has shown me that our need for love cannot be met by other people alone. We need more. I've seen it again and again in people's vain attempts to fill their hearts with a series of lovers, friends, husbands, and wives.

Don't get me wrong - we need one another. We need friends, husbands, and wives. We are built for relationships. We need to experience their love and share our love with them. But no matter how well we love others or they love us, there is a deeper need.

We need to know we are loved just as we are; personally; deeply, unconditionally - and the only source of that love is God. He's the only one with the proper perspective: Creator.

The Creator God loves you as only a Creator can: personally, deeply, unconditionally, and completely. He knows how you were made, why you were made, your successes and your failures, and what you truly need. He knows your thoughts, ideas, and desires from every angle. He knows the depth, the width, and the eternal.

Why?

It may strike you as odd that I've put a section about God in the middle of this book. It is not.

This is not a section about God. I did not write this section to prove the existence of the Creator of the Universe. He doesn't need my help, and whether or not you choose to believe in Him is entirely up to you.

This is a section about you. It is a section about the realities of your life on this planet: your questions, needs, and struggles; questions that you've been told not to ask, needs that you've been told will never be met and therefore shouldn't matter; and struggles that appear never ending and meaningless.

It is a section about the realities of your life on this planet.

The questions are real and the answers are good. We all have them because we are all a part of The Great Story - a story of adventures, battles, and love that are yours to be lived.

Your needs will be met because you matter. Your adventures, battles, and loves are not just for you. We all benefit from your success.

Yes, the struggles are indeed never-ending, but they are never meaningless.

The struggles are meaningful because they defeat a wrong. Don't miss this point. The wrongs will continue unless we're willing to fight them. The problems of this world will never stop unless we each do our part to solve them. Large or small, temporary or permanent, minor or life changing, all struggles are battles between right and wrong.

The struggles are meaningful because they make you better. Just like exercise strengthens muscle, the struggles of your life make you stronger, healthier, and more capable. They also increase your capacity and therefore, your usefulness.

> # The glory of God is man fully alive.
> ## - St. Irenaeus

As you see yourself able to handle more struggles successfully, you'll seek out more; and not just more of them, but the more important ones. This creates a powerful cycle of success and growth that benefits the world and you. Bigger problems get solved and you live fully alive.

So, maybe this is a section about God after all. Maybe it's one long encouragement for you to get to know Him more so you can connect your questions, needs, and struggles with the ultimate Adventurer, Warrior, and Lover. Personally, I believe that'd be a good thing.

Be Unique

I believe that would be a good thing because it will help you to be you - a confident, purpose-full you with a solid understanding of what it is you're doing with your life. It would also make you a star in most people's eyes.

Here's what I mean.

Second only to the myth about talent, the most commonly discussed myth in the music and entertainment industry states that you have to be unique in order to succeed. This myth has given us an endless parade of outrageous singers, bands, and songs over the years.

I'm not saying uniqueness doesn't work, because it often does. Many of those outrageous singers, bands, and songs were successful, for a while. A few have had long term careers and most have been forgotten. They were hot and they were gone.

Then there's U2.

Formed in 1976 when the members were in high school, U2 is considered one of the top acts in Music. They've sold over 150 million records, have won 22 Grammy Awards, more than any other band, and are ranked by Rolling Stone magazine at number 22 in its list of the "100 Greatest Artists of All Time."

The reason I bring them up is that it would be easy to mistake their uniqueness as the key to their success. Especially when you consider the number of times they have reinvented their music, image, and causes they have supported during their 30-plus year career. It would be easy to see them as an example of how you have to "stay ahead of public tastes" in order to be a success.

But U2 is not a success because they've chased public tastes. U2 is a success because they've passionately lived who they are: a creative and curious group of musicians with a desire to change the world.

The passionate life they've lived has made them stars because people are drawn to passion. This is why uniqueness in itself never works; it's fake. People don't want fake, they want truth, authenticity, and passion. They want life.

They want you.

Be You (the two most important words in this book)

I said earlier that people don't buy things; they buy solutions. I also said that people always have two reasons for their decisions: the one they tell you and the real one.

> Don't ask what the world needs. Ask what makes you come alive, because what the world needs is people who have come alive.
>
> — **Howard Thurman**

I'll now add that the real one is always emotional.

It's always emotional because people are living breathing creatures not robots. We are designed to connect, and we connect through emotions.

The easiest and only real way to connect with people is to be yourself - the *you* that's designed to accomplish great things through your art.

There is nothing more important than knowing what makes you come alive. Not only will it save you from spending years searching, chasing and grasping, it will connect you with people and give you a life.

Your life.

And isn't that ultimately what you want?

CHAPTER 9

You, Inc.

When I first said you own a business and it's YOU back in chapter 4, I gave you - the CEO of You, Inc. - a list of items you needed to consider in order to run a successful business.

Here's that list with a quick summary of each item:

- **You, Inc. needs a mission** - a clear idea of where you're going and why.

- **You, Inc. needs a board of directors** - a team of trusted advisors. It doesn't matter if it's a formal group or not, or whether you meet as a group or not. The important thing is that you have a group of people to help you reach your goals.
- **You, Inc. needs a product** - your product is the unique combination of you and your art.
- **You, Inc. needs goals** - the life you want to live and how your career fits with, and supports, that life.
- **You, Inc. needs a business plan** - everything in this list put together into action steps and "to dos."
- **You, Inc. needs a marketing strategy** - how you're going to make connections with fans and potential fans.
- **You, Inc. needs customers** - who you're going to connect with.
- **You, Inc. needs a sales team** - this could be people who work for you, your materials and what you do online, or fans.
- **You, Inc. needs capital** - money.
- **You, Inc. needs to be profitable** - money.
- **You, Inc. needs a building** - (a roof over your head, food and clothing) in other words, the things money will buy.
- **(There was a nap, too)**

The last three items on the list are about money. Capital is a technical term for money that is used to start a business - buying tools and materials and paying employees. Profits are the money that's left over after all the business bills are paid and that includes the costs of shelter, food and clothing.

Plan your work...

work your plan.

- **Norman Vincent Peale**

I purposely skipped the subject of money until now. You had to first understand "everything that is important" to you. Now that you have a clear idea of the career and life you want, we can talk about how to pay for it.

Money

Let's talk about air.

Air is something we don't think about much. We don't earn air; it is simply "there" all the time. It's only after we run too fast and start gasping that we are aware of our need for it at all.

Until our air is cut off.

Suddenly, air is important. As we start really gasping for it, air becomes the only thing on our minds. If air is not given to us we begin to panic, which only makes matters worse since there's nothing we can do. We can't earn more, but we panic anyway.

> # Money is not the most important thing in life, but money does affect everything that is important.
> ### - Kim Kiyosaki

And in severe cases, of course, we die.

The same things happen when our money supply is cut off.

When money is cut off, we grasp for it. We begin to budget and "think twice" about a cup of coffee or new CD. We begin to panic and say "How am I going to pay my bills?" and, "Can you lend me some money this week?"

In severe cases we die, but that usually doesn't happen. Instead, we get a job - any job. Because we're panicking and we CAN earn more money, we take any job we can find.

We work hard to solve our money problems, but we're trapped; trapped in the job that we didn't truly want and trapped by the fear of

NOT having that job. We're trapped between the need for money and how we want to live our life.

I just described extreme cases where money - and air - are cut off suddenly, causing life threatening problems. Thankfully, cases like those are rare. Sadly, the following is not:

Living the Dream

Consider the story of two college-graduate newlyweds. In addition to joining their lives, they are also combining their student loans, a few credit cards, and at least one car payment.

They aren't worried about the bills though, because they both have good jobs. In fact, combining their incomes has given them more money than they've ever seen before. They start to pay down their loans and cards, and they still have money left over.

So, they buy a house.

They are happy with their purchase because the house payment is about the same as the money they were paying in rent. This all fits their plan, but they have one problem: part of the house is empty because it's twice the size of their apartment. They see an ad on TV promising furniture with no payments or interest for two years, and off they go. Problem solved.

Until they have a baby, which wasn't part of the plan. They are both already working so hard to pay for their debt and lifestyle. This isn't what they wanted. Back when they got married, they promised each other that their baby would not grow up in a daycare.

But they're trapped. It wasn't a sudden cut off of money. It was a long, slow build up of bills and debt. But the end result is the same: people who are trapped between the need for money and how they want to live their lives.

They have not died physically, but they have died a little in their soul. They have died because they are now working for money instead of pursuing their life's passion. They are merely breathing, not living.

You do not have to live that life.

You don't have to let money trap you. It doesn't have special powers, and it isn't evil or good. Money is nothing more than a tool that's used to buy the things we need for life.

Money is a tool you can control - if you learn how and why it works.

There are two reasons you don't know these things already.

One, personal money management is not taught in most schools and is rarely discussed by parents. You may have learned a little here and there through experience, but you've not been taught.

Two, what little you have been taught has been from banks. I'm not saying their information is a lie, but beware that banks make money based on what you, the customer, know and don't know. After all, banks are in business to make money, too. They have a product to sell, and most of the information they give you is slanted in their favor.

Don't worry, though, There are many ways you can learn about money. There are many excellent books, magazines, blogs, and podcasts you can use. It is not a difficult subject and you only need 3rd grade math skills to manage your growing fortune.

You also don't have to forget your passions to earn the money you need. Like I said in Chapter One, it is possible to earn money in the arts. By learning how to control money instead of allowing it to control you, you'll be able to pursue any career you want and still have food and shelter.

Before I give you the basics, please understand I am not an expert. These are the things I believe you need to know, but I am not a Certified Public Accountant, a tax advisor, or an attorney. You need people with that kind of knowledge in your life if you are going to succeed. Make sure you have them on your Board of Directors.

Money has no value

Thousands of years ago, people traded what they had for what they needed. If they had milk and needed eggs, they traded milk for eggs. If they had eggs and needed their roof fixed, they traded eggs for the work.

But what if you had the eggs, but you didn't need milk or your roof fixed? What then?

Man created money.

Instead of taking the milk, which they didn't need, the person with the eggs would take a promissory note. The note said "1 gallon of milk" and was a promise to give whoever had the note a gallon of milk. The holder of the note (the egg guy) could then exchange that note for what they needed, like a fixed roof.

Soon, people began exchanging the notes themselves but instead of milk, the notes had the value of the milk ($5.00 for instance). In other words, people began exchanging money.

It's important to note that money has no value in and of itself. Money is nothing more than a promissory note - a piece of paper or a coin - that we *say* is worth $5.00. It is meaningless by itself. It is only worth $5.00 because everyone in the system agrees it is worth $5.00.

This is important for two reasons:

1. Because money has no value by itself, its value is always changing. This is why something that costs $5.00 one day might cost $6.00 tomorrow, or $4.00. It all depends on the value society gives the money or the items themselves.

2. There is a limitless supply of money. This is probably the hardest part of money to understand. Unlike gold and silver, or natural resources of any kind, society makes more money when it is needed. Why would more be needed? There are many reasons, but I want to talk about only one: inventions. The act of inventing (and making music is a form of invention) creates something of value out of thin air. Money is printed to allow for growth like this. Note: printing money causes some problems that are beyond the scope of what we are discussing here.

Many of the biggest challenges in life, both personally and in society as a whole, are based on the mistaken belief that the only way to make money is to take from someone else. But I've just explained why that's wrong.

Your desires for a job, money, or success do not mean that others have to do without. In fact, the opposite is true. If, as I said, the money supply grows when value is created, then the creation of value has to be a good thing. Not only does it add it's initial value, but it increases the available money for everyone.

Earning Money

I've already mentioned that there are three things you can do with money: you can earn it, spend it, or invest it. There are multiple ways you can do all three. I'll just cover the basics here.

There are two types of earned income: active or passive. Active income is money that's earned according to how much time you work or how many things you do. Most jobs in the world pay active income. Passive income is money that's earned over and over again after the initial work is done. Screenwriting is an example of work that leads to passive income. Novelists write their novel once but they are paid every time someone buys the book. Sometimes this income can come in for years and years.

Active Income (work = money)	Passive Income (work = ongoing money)
Use a job - make money - get experience	Create an "asset" - write a song - play on a record
Create a job - form a band - give lessons	Buy an "asset" - buy a recording studio - invest in a 401K - buy a rental house

Spending Money

Though decisions about spending money are sometimes about good or bad, they are usually about need vs. want and down or up.

Need vs. want:
Many people get into trouble because they confuse wants for needs and buy way too much stuff they can't afford and never use. Is what you want to buy a need or a want? There are three answers to this question, and three appropriate responses.
   1. It's a need. Buy it.
   2. It's a want and you can afford it. Buy it.
   3. It's a want and you can't afford it or you're not sure. Wait, which is always a good option.

Down or up:
Ask yourself if what you're buying is going to go down or up in value. Clothing, electronics and cars are examples of things that go down in value. This is called depreciation. Houses, jewelry and some musical instruments appreciate, or go up in value - sometimes, but not always. Just consider the North American housing market for the last few years. Houses, which traditionally have appreciated in value, have been going down in value.

Before I talk about investing, I want to discuss the biggest spending challenge for most artists: equipment and supplies. I know this well because I struggled with it my whole career.

I struggled because the answer to whether a new drum was a need or a want was, "Yes." The value question didn't help either because I knew - or wanted to believe - that the new drum would help me get more work.

I don't have an easy answer to this challenge, but I will give you ideas that will help in a few moments. For now, know that the answer depends not only on these answers, but on how your life and career are going when you're trying to decide.

Investing Money

This is my definition of investing: putting your money to work making you more money.

The best example of this is an interest bearing savings account, which is also the most basic of financial investments. What makes it an investment is the term "interest bearing" which means that the bank will pay you to use your money while it sits in your account.

Let's say you put $100.00 in the savings account. The bank will lend that money to people who need it and pay you 1 to 2% per year as a thank you. They get more customers and the money they earn on the loan and you get a safe place for your money plus 1 or 2 dollars while doing nothing. You've just earned some passive income.

Making 1 to 2%, or a dollar or two a year, isn't much. But then, neither is a $100.00 investment. There are ways to make a higher percentage of interest and better places than savings accounts to put money, but you have to first ask yourself the spending questions of need vs. want and down or up. These questions apply to investing because investing is a form of spending. It's a better way of spending, but it is spending nonetheless.

- Need vs. want: The simple answer is that you need to invest - everybody does. There will come a day when you won't be able to work but you'll still need to eat. Proper investments could save your life. This doesn't mean that everyone *can* invest. If you don't have enough money, investing is a want.

- Down or up: This is THE investment question because no one wants their investments to go down and everyone wants them to go up, up, UP! If the answers were easy everyone would be a millionaire. When you're ready to invest, hire a professional recommended by people on your Board of Directors.

The right professional will guide you to the right investments and the right *kinds* of investments. They'll help you decide on the amount of interest you'd like verses the risks. They'll also help you learn about and decide between financial investments and business investments - owning a business, but not running it.

Keep your money

The end goal of personal finance should always be to keep as much of your money as ethically and legally possible. I do not mean this in the sense of cheating or greed. I mean it in the sense of responsibility; a responsibility that runs both ways.

The "world system" - people, money, business, laws (taxes) - has a responsibility to follow the rules. These rules have been agreed upon and work pretty well for most people. You, in turn, have a responsibility to play by those rules and do your part.

You do your part in two ways: the work you do and what you do with your rewards. The work you do should benefit the world as we've discussed in this book. It should also benefit the world financially as you buy stuff, hire people, and pay your taxes.

Your rewards should also benefit the world as you share them as you see fit. Whether that's extra time, food, or money doesn't matter. What matters is that it benefits others - another part of having something to work for that's bigger than yourself.

But you can only give out of what you have. That's why I say you have a responsibility to keep as much of your money as ethically and legally possible. The more you keep, the more time, food, and/or money you can share.

A Lifetime Plan

How long do you plan on eating?

Do you plan on eating through tomorrow night at 11:00, until the end of next week, or for the rest of your life? How long would you like to have clothes and a place to live? Are these things you'd like to have for a month, or would you like to enjoy them until you die?

The answer to these questions is the same, right? Eating, clothing and shelter are all "rest of your life" issues. They are ongoing needs that will never end.

Make sure your money plan is "rest of your life," too. It doesn't make sense to focus on short term solutions - the next job or gig - while trying to solve the long term problems of food and shelter.

Cash Flow

If keeping as much of your money is the end goal of personal finance, then having cash flow is how you make the goal. It is an accounting term that means pretty much what it sounds like: the flow of cash in and through your budget.

In the case of cash flow, the cash doesn't mean dollars and loose change. It means usable money whether it's in cash, in a checking account, or in quickly accessible savings. It is also not a term that means a certain amount, as if to say "Make sure you have $1,000 cash flow each month."

The easiest way to explain cash flow, and it's importance, is to talk about bad cash flow. An example of bad cash flow would be working a job today that is going to pay you $1,500 in 2 months, having no money in the bank, and having $650 for rent and utilities due next Monday.

That is called negative cash flow - more money going out than coming in. The problem with negative cash flow is, it is a problem today that needed a solution yesterday.

Positive cash flow, on the other hand, is about finding the financial solutions today for problems that will happen tomorrow. It is about managing your life, your work, your spending, and investing so that you always have money coming in when or before you need it - and if possible, more money than you need.

Nothing will kill your career faster than negative cash flow.

It will kill your career because you will struggle to have the equipment, materials and other tools you need to succeed. Those things matter. Trust me on this one.

It will kill you because you will burn out from the constant struggle of paying your bills, finding jobs/gigs, hunting down pay (which you will sometimes never get), and not having money for a life.

Negative cash flow will also make everyone think you're begging and harassing people for work - and it will be true. You will be desperate and they will know it. They will then wonder why you don't work enough. This will cause them to not hire you because they'll assume you're not good at what you do.

I did all three, and they killed my career. It was ugly, painful, and self-destructive. I didn't know any better at the time, but so what? Now you know. What are going to do about it?

My suggestion is to be serious about your financial education. Learn how to control money or it will control you. Money may not have any special powers, but it affects everything important to life - negatively and positively. Learning to control it will help you have more of the positive.

Get a Job

I also suggest you get a job. I say this for a couple of reasons. First, taking the wrong artistic work is more destructive than working a part-time job flipping burgers. No one in the creative arts will think you're confused about whether you want to be an artist or a cook. Everyone will be confused if you take a gig that's outside of what you want to do.

Second, you can learn a lot in "real world" jobs. A waiter job will help you deal with difficult people and think on your feet. A job at an entertainment industry company will help you understand the business and legal side of the arts. A job in sales will help you sell yourself as an artist. All jobs will help you to understand others, and how non-creatives earn a living.

Don't just take any job. That's a waste of time and a lost opportunity. You're number one focus in getting a job should be the things you can learn on that job. Things that will help you pursue the career and life you want. The money must be the second focus, or you'll trap yourself in the comfort of a nice paycheck, referred to by some as "golden handcuffs."

The Plan

Now that you have a basic understanding of money, we can get back to the plan. But the actual plan is worthless if you never use it, and you'll never use your plan if it's based on the list in this book.

There's nothing wrong with the list. I'm glad we've used it as a way to learn. But if you fill in all the details completely, you'll never read it again. That isn't a slam against you, it's what happens with big and complicated plans.

Most businesses I've worked with never look at their plans after they're done. That doesn't mean the work of making them was a waste of time, but it does mean that the plan doesn't help the business as much as it could.

No amount of planning will help you succeed in life if you don't use your plan. Without use, your plan will become another stack of paper or computer files taking up space in your life. Other than making you mad every time you see them, the papers and files won't accomplish anything.

To help you out, I've gotten rid of all the big words and combined the necessary pieces into five parts: your Board of Directors, Vision/Mission, Goals, Marketing, and Money. I've put them all on a nice, neat form on the next page.

The Business Plan of You, Inc.

Section One - My Board

List the people on your board and/or the people you WANT on your board

_____   _____   _____

_____   _____   _____

_____   _____   _____

Section Two - Vision/Mission

*Write what it is you're going to do - Vision - and
how you're going to do it - Mission*

Section Three - Goals

The specific things you'll achieve along the way

1.   4.   7.

2.   5.   8.

3.   6.   9.

Section Four - Marketing Plan

Your product, your customers, your message and "branding."

Section Five - Money Plan

How you'll earn your money, how much, and what you'll do with it too.

Once you fill in that plan, or make something similar, you'll need a way to make sure you use it - regularly. I suggest you keep your plan HANDY - Handy, Accountable, Nearly Right, Daily, and Focused on the Why.

Handy

Your plan should be easy to find in less than one or two steps. Don't leave it out where everyone can read it, but don't hide it either. Burying it in a drawer or deep inside your computer won't help you at all. Bumping into it a few times a week will.

Still, it's not enough to just bump into it. You have to schedule reviews. For reasons you'll see in a moment, the whole plan should be read at least twice a year. Mark your calendar so you don't forget. Other parts that include specific action steps should be reviewed every couple of months.

These reviews are crucial if you want to succeed. As hard as it may be to believe, you will forget most of what you've planned for yourself without timely reviews. Time and distractions will win unless you stay focused on your plan.

Accountable

Another surefire way to stay focused is to let other people help you. There's nothing more motivating than the knowledge that you'll have to tell a friend or family member how you're doing. Make this work in your favor by sharing your plan - or parts of it - with carefully chosen people in your life.

Choose carefully and wisely, your life depends on it. Choose a few and share everything, or share pieces with a few more. Either way, the details of your plan are NOT to be shared with everyone. Choose people you care about and who care about you. There must be skin in the game or it won't work. It's likely these people will be the same people as your Board of Directors, but they don't have to be.

Ask these people to ask you about how you're working your plan. When they ask, tell them honestly or this won't work.

Check on how this relationship is working and change it if: (a) it's not working, or (b) it's threatening your friendship. Remember, what you want is a life, and a life without friends and family is not a life.

Nearly Right

In order for your plan to work, it must be believable and you will soon realize yours is not. Here's why:

- Your plan is wrong - No matter how careful you've been, you've missed or misunderstood important steps and/or goals. Everybody does.
- You're wrong - You don't know enough to make a perfect plan and your plan is only as good as the information you have. Don't worry, you'll learn more.
- You'll change - Even some of your most passionate beliefs and desires will change in the years to come. No one stays the same forever (and that's a good thing).

Recognize that there will be a day when you'll review your plan and think, "What was I thinking?" Whether that day is tomorrow or next year doesn't matter, what matters is that you know your plan should be "nearly right."

Nearly right is good enough and it's all you'll ever have. You will drive yourself crazy making a perfect plan, so don't. Allow your plan to be nearly right and keep going.

On the other hand, if something can and should be updated, do it. Your plan should be what they call a "living document" - constantly changing as the facts change. Updating your plan will keep it believable and keep it used.

Be flexible. Recognize that your plan and your goals will change over time. Having this in mind will keep you using the plan you have while giving you the freedom to update it along the way.

A nearly right plan is one that is both usable and believable. It's usable because it makes enough sense to follow while allowing for the flexibility to deal with the unexpected. It's believable because it's reviewed and changed to deal with the unexpected.

Daily

Your plan must be worked on a daily basis.

It's up to you whether that means 5, 6 or 7 days a week (I do not recommend 7). Do something everyday, and not just anything, but specific things that move yourself closer towards your goals.

> How am I going to live today in order to create the tomorrow I'm committed to?
>
> - Tony Robbins

Plan your daily actions and goals for each day. Some people find it best to do this the night before and others have more success at the beginning of each day. Figure out what works best for you and make that planning time part of your regular schedule.

- Plan "habit" tasks: things you have to do every day, like practicing your art.
- Plan the other tasks in order of priority of need or importance.
- Plan your life stuff in there too. You need to pay your bills, so put paying your bills on your list.

- Don't overdo it. A daily list with 20 items is overwhelming and depressing. You'll be lucky if you accomplish anything at all. When in doubt, go small. You can always do more.
- Learn when, where, and how you work best. Everyone has peak times of productivity during the day. Mine are from 7:00 to 11:00 AM and 4:00 to 8:00 PM each day. They are not always the most convenient times to work, but I try to hit them as much as I can. I also work better in some places than others. So do you.
- Plan down time or down time will kill your list. You will take this time whether you plan it or not so you may as well plan it. You'll also find you'll be more productive if you take frequent breaks. Really.

Not only do daily goals keep you moving forward, they give you successes and focus. At the end of everyday you'll have a solid achievement for that day and you'll have thought about your plan all day long.

Focused on the Why

There's one more thing you can do to help you put your plan into action: Focus on the Why by putting reminders about your plan everywhere in your life. Here's how it works.

First, keep an eye out for pictures, ads, words, and encouragements that most remind you of your dreams. It doesn't matter where you find them; photo albums, websites, magazines, whatever. When you see them, grab 'em or save them on your computer if you can.

Next, place them where you'll see them everyday. Places like your bathroom or bedroom mirrors, computer and phone screensavers, or your refrigerator door and cork board. The point is to have them in and around your life so you see them all the time.

Just as with other parts of the plan, be thoughtful about what's public and what's not. If anyone sees a picture and asks, tell 'em proudly that it's there to remind you of something you'll have one day.

Keep your plan HANDY: Handy, Accountable, Nearly right, Daily and Focused on the Why.

Enjoy the Process

Congratulations, you now have a plan based on a deeper understanding of your art, the world of business, and how the two fit together. You know you have lots more to learn, but have the tools and the self knowledge to learn what you need. You also know how. Most importantly, you have a greater knowledge about who you are, what you are capable of, and what you'd like to pursue.

I encourage you to enjoy the victories, both big and small. In fact, be sure to enjoy the small ones. There will be far more of those and the celebrations will keep you - and your friends and family - motivated along the way.

Yes, take time to celebrate the victories. Throw parties, tell friends, tell the press, buy or do something nice for yourself.

Celebrate.

I also encourage you to accept, and at least try to enjoy, your failures, too. They will come, and you must be prepared. Understand that they are how we learn - if we take the time to study them. So, study them. Learn from your mistakes, and only make those mistakes once.

Enjoy the process, for that is where life is found. Victories and failures give our emotions the reasons to prove we're alive. Count all the experiences as the blessings they are and then move on. More and better blessings are around the next corner.

One final quote:

Today, you have 100% of your life left.

- Tom Landry

Go work your plan. Live fully alive.

RESOURCES

FAILED

As a creative, you have spent time and money perfecting your art.

You've taken lessons, gone to performances and exhibits, read about and watched the masters, and practiced, practiced, practiced. You've done this because you know that it takes time and effort to get great at what you do.

If I've done my job through this book, you now know that you need more than artistic skills to succeed in the arts. You know that talent is not enough, that you need a big "why," and you know the basics of

"real world" information that will help you build your career.
But there's much more to learn.

It's my hope that you'll devote the time and effort needed to get great
at the business side of your career too. I hope that you'll use the ladder
over the wall between the arts and the real world and become a student
of business like you've been a student of your craft.

This chapter will show you how.

Over the Wall

The Grammy Awards took place last night and there's one thing I
know: all the TV coverage today will be about who was wearing what.
It's the same with the Oscars, Emmys and Tonys too: endless coverage
of fashion with little to no mention of what it takes to win an award.

With few exceptions, it is difficult to find anything on TV, radio, or
online that covers anything having to do with building a successful
artistic career.

Visit the arts section of a bookstore in person or online and it's
difficult to find anything about business principles applied to your
career. You can learn some of them through biographies, but that's
about it. Most of the books in the arts section are celebrations of
already successful artists that focus on - you guessed it - talent and
luck.

The few creative arts business books that exist are about the things I
said I wouldn't cover in this book: the listing of publishers, managers,
agents, advice about contracts, performance techniques, and how to do
your hair and make-up.

Do you need that information? Yes. Do you need to learn about the
artistic side of the arts? Yes. Do you need to keep taking lessons,

going to performances and exhibits, reading about and watching the masters, and practicing? Yes.

To learn more about business though, you'll have to look somewhere else. You'll have to climb the ladder over the wall and go to the real world. You will find it to be a world that is FULL of the information you need to build your career.

This is the world that taught me what I know, the world that gave me my "Ah ha" moments and the answers to my questions. The "Real World" is the world that led me to write this book for you.

It's time for you to explore this world on your own. It's time to look at the books, magazines, websites, blogs, seminars, and classes of the real world and see what they have for you.

Connections

If you've never looked over this wall before, I can tell you from experience it will be intimidating. There are thousands of new business books written every year, hundreds of thousands of blogs and websites to read, and an endless supply of "expert gurus" ready and willing to take all the money you have.

There are two ways you can cut through the noise to find the information that's right for you. You're already familiar with one of them, but the second will take a little practice.

First, ask for recommendations and rely on people you can trust. This is something you already do every day with your craft. You use recommendations from a group of friends and fellow creatives to help you find the hottest art as soon as it appears.

It's no different with business information. Start with people you trust - your board - and ask them for advice on both what you should be reading/watching and also who else you should trust for advice. In a short time you'll have a network you can rely on.

Second, train yourself to look for:

- Connections *for* your dream. Look for the gaps between what you need to know and what you already know. Do you need help in marketing? Close that gap by reading about marketing. Be on the lookout for information and resources that give you support *for* your dream and connect the two together.
- Connections *to* your dream: Look for connections to your dream in everything you read, hear, and learn. If a connection *for* your dream is about actively looking for information, connections *to* your dream are found through creative thinking.

Here's an example:

In a recent issue of Fast Company magazine, there was a story about a new kind of city called an Aerotropolis - a city built around an airport. Man has always built cities around transportation: New Orleans was built for ships and Chicago was built for trains, so this is the next logical step.

If you're wondering why this hasn't happened before, it's because we haven't had the Internet, so many small gadgets, or global supply chains before.

The internet has connected businesses all over the world. More than 40% of what's made in the world is now small enough that it can be delivered in an airplane. Put those two together and you get businesses that are linked together to form supply chains, like Dell Computers.

Most of Dell's computer parts aren't even made until an order comes in. Once an order is placed, businesses all over the world make and then ship the specific parts - by airplane. Once the parts arrive at the assembly plant, they are put together, boxed up and shipped - by airplane - directly to the customer.

An Aerotropolis is designed to make supply chains like this even faster and cheaper.

At the center of the Aerotropolis will be the airport itself. The first ring of buildings surrounding the airport will be warehouses and shipping companies. The next ring will have big and small manufacturing plants as well as general business offices. The people of these cities will live far from the airport in the outside ring where there will be houses and apartments, shopping centers, schools, parks, clubs, and restaurants.

So, how is an article about an Aerotropolis connected to your dream?

I think the biggest connection is the lesson about supply chains. Business is, and always will be, about supply chains. Supply chains have affected all of world history, too. The reason the United States was "discovered" was because Columbus was looking for a better link in a supply chain for Portugal.

Do you know what's at the heart of the current messes in the music and entertainment industries? Two words – supply chains.

The huge entertainment companies were built to deliver products to consumers. From finding artists and recording their music, to making VHS tapes or DVDs, to shipping product to stores, the entire business model was about moving stuff and collecting money along the way.

The Internet took most of the links in that supply chain away and the se companies have been trying to adapt ever since.

Another connection to your dream (maybe) is how and where people will be living in the future. Giant Aerotropolises will have millions and millions of people that will want to be entertained. There will be huge demand for:

- Local artists that reflect the cities and the culture.
- New club and concert venues in the outer ring.
- Touring support for acts, shows and exhibits coming into and going out of the city.
- Other support businesses for all that goes into creative productions: equipment, product manufacturing and shipping, management, etc.
- Radio/Internet broadcasts with local flavor.

From this extreme example of a crazy thing called an Aerotroplis, I've given you two connections to your career: information about supply chains and cities where you might want to live.

This should make you think about your own supply chains. What are the links? How can you make them stronger? Are there some that could be, or will be, taken out, and how can you prepare?

What about living in an Aerotropolis? Is that a good fit for you? How could you learn more about where they're being built? If you don't want to move, are there changes going on in your city that are connected to this concept; things like where and how buildings are being built and why? Are any of these changes creating opportunities for you?

If you stay open to learning every time you read, you'll find connections, too. Remember that change *always* brings opportunities, so be on the lookout for what they are.

Books

I love books. They give you one-on-one access to the thoughts and ideas of some of the most brilliant people in the world for around $20.00 (or free if you use the library).

I know books can be scary because of their size, or maybe because of bad experiences from school, but please check them out. Search around online and talk to people you trust. You'll be surprised how much you'll actually like reading when you're learning about something that will help you and your career.

I recommend you look for books in three categories: self-development, money, and business. Self-development books will cover topics such as people skills, communication, and networking. Look for money books that discuss either personal finances or business finances, these will help you learn how to make money and how to keep more of it.

The broadest of these three categories will be business. Look for business books that focus on marketing, entrepreneurialism (business startups), and leadership. These will give you not only the information you need as CEO of You, Inc., but also insight into the attitudes and perspectives of others who are in business for themselves.

You don't have to stick with "how to" books either. Biographies are full of useful information, while being tremendously entertaining, too. Look for the reasons behind why the person did what they did and you'll find plenty to use in your career.

When reading books, it's important to know that you may not always like what you read. That's okay. Just as in art, some authors are better and more entertaining than others. If a book is a pain to read, get another one on the same subject.

If reading the book isn't a pain, but you don't like what the author's saying, keep reading. Why? Because when you're done, you'll have _two_ ideas on the subject. You might not use the second one, but that extra idea will help you make better and stronger decisions for yourself.

This is no different than how you already grow artistically. It doesn't matter whether you love the art you're involved with or not. Everything you see and hear becomes a part of who you are and makes you a better artist.

Magazines

Don't have time for books? Read magazines. In fact, even if you have time for books, I still recommend you read business magazines. They are quicker to read, have more timely information, and are interesting because the stories are about people's lives.

Subscribe to two or three that write the way you like and have a good mix of articles and interviews.

I suggest you read every issue cover to cover, including the ads. This will help you keep in touch with the rapid pace of change in the world; change that will affect entertainment, technology, marketing, advertising, and sales. Keeping up with these changes will help you spot and take advantage of the opportunities you'll need.

The Internet

For the same reasons I'm a fan of magazines, I recommend you check out business blogs, websites, and newsletters. Not only will you find more brilliant minds delivering their latest and greatest ideas, you can learn from them in two to five minute chunks.

Two things to be aware of:
1. The internet is like a bathroom wall: anyone can write anything. Be aware that there's a huge amount of junk online.
2. The internet can also be an extreme time-sucking machine. It's easy to get lost and suddenly realize it's been hours since you looked at the clock. Make sure that the time spent is productive

and efficient. Remember, where you'll be in five years depends on what you're doing today.

The best way to handle these two problems is to learn about and use the available tools, especially RSS and Twitter.

RSS, or Real Simple Syndication, is a technology that sends blog posts and website updates directly to you. This means you can go to one place online, read the latest info, and move on with your day. This is not only fast, but it avoids the dangers of endless surfing.

I know there's a lot of controversy about Twitter, but I find it a powerful information source because I follow people who either write about what I need to know or read about what I need to know. If you do the same, your Twitter feed will be full of the most up to date and important information online. You'll be able to click on the links, learn a bunch, and move on with your day.

All of the resources I've talked about so far have involved reading. Now it's time to discuss training courses, seminars and/or classes offered by adult education companies, specialists, and even colleges and universities where you live.

Training Courses

One of the things I learned in the corporate world is how much companies invest in giving their employees the skills, knowledge and practice they need to succeed. These companies know that knowledgeable employees will do their jobs better and longer, too.

Though some companies train their own employees, most of them pay for training programs given by adult education businesses. Many of these businesses offer courses to the public as well. I recommend you see what's available near you.

Just like with reading, look for courses in marketing,

entrepreneurialism, and leadership. I also suggest one more: public speaking. Not only will this help you directly when you're performing, but it will give you confidence whenever you talk with people in person.

An organization I highly recommend is Dale Carnegie Training. Started by author, teacher, and speaker, Dale Carnegie, in 1913, this global organization offers one of the best courses you can take: Effective Communications & Human Relations. Like the name says, it is a class that teaches you how to communicate with and work with people.

Note: I am a certified Dale Carnegie Facilitator but I do not earn money from referrals.

New Horizons is another company that specializes in adult education. They are located in many cities and offer a complete list of classes covering a wide variety of subjects that will help your career.

If formal training seems a bit much, consider joining Toastmasters. Toastmasters is made up of people who want to get better at speaking in public. They hold weekly meetings where everyone gives a speech and receives encouraging reviews from the rest of the group.

Most towns have Toastmaster meetings and many have them at multiple times and locations. The last time I checked in the Nashville, Tennessee area, there were over 30 different meetings going on around town. Chances are there are quite a few around your town, too. Look in the yellow pages, or the meetings and announcement sections of your local paper.

Classes

Most colleges and universities have adult education classes designed for people like you - people that want specific information to help them in their careers. Some will allow you to take regular classes even if you're not a full-time student. This can be an inexpensive way to learn finance, marketing, graphics, music, speech, etc.

Colleges and universities often open their doors to the public when visiting speakers are on campus. These free events are a terrific way to learn about new topics. Be on the lookout for other learning opportunities from campus concerts or special events.

Seminars

Have you ever stayed up and watched late night television? Late enough to see the _"Come to this one day seminar and learn how you can buy real estate with no money down!"_ commercials? I certainly don't suggest them all, but there are things to be learned from these types of business meetings, too.

There are two major advantages to these short gatherings: One, they are (usually) cheap in terms of both time and money. Two, they are very focused and can be a quick way to learn a lot.

Be aware that some of these will try to get you to buy or signup for something before they let you leave. Don't let that scare you from learning useful information the rest of the day.

Lifetime Learning

I hope you will seek out and take advantage of the resources I've talked about in this chapter. They will help to remind you that you own a business - and it's you - and encourage you to be the best owner and CEO of that business you can be.

They will also help you to become a lifelong learner, which is perhaps the greatest skill you can have. It will help you keep pace with an ever changing world, and it will increase your self-confidence.

There are two parts of becoming a lifelong learner. The first is to have the will to learn. It's not enough to want to learn, or need to learn, or even know you can learn. You have to move yourself forward to the point of acting on the statement, "I *will* learn." Once you're at that point, it's simply a matter of finding the right resource or tool.

The second part of becoming a lifelong learner is knowing how to learn. Some of us (me) learn by reading. Others learn by hearing. Still others learn from watching and doing. Likewise, some people learn best in short bursts while others have to be engaged for hours on end. Take the time to figure out what works best for you and stick to it.

Please keep in mind that (a) you can learn and (b) HOW you learn only matters to you. I say this because you are probably part of the high percentage of people who do not learn the way schools teach. If that's true, it's also probably true that you felt like a failure - or worse - for at least the first 18 years of your life.

You are not.

The only thing those first 18 years prove is that you do not learn the way that most schools teach. Most schools rely on words to teach students which is a method called *verbal linguistic*. People who learn through words do well in school. In fact, many of them do so well they choose careers as - yep - teachers.

Don't let how you did in school - good or bad - have anything to do with your adult choice to be a lifelong learner. This is one of the best things about all the information in the real world - it's available anyway you need it (including information about learning styles, too.)

This is one reason I have not given you a specific list of books and websites in this chapter. You need to figure out what kind of resources will work best for you, not me.

I do have the following exceptions though. I have a list of seven things I believe in so much that I have to mention them here. Even within the list, note that you can still choose how you want to use them - whether to read or listen to the books for instance.

My personal recommendations:

Books
- ***How to Win Friends and Influence People* by Dale Carnegie** - Considered the number one book on how to work and live with people for over 70 years. If you read only one book, this should be the one. It's full of interesting stories and usable tips. Read it yearly, highlight it and keep it handy - yes, it's that important.
- ***Personality Plus* by Florence Littauer** - The easiest to understand, and therefore most usable study of the 4 basic personality styles found in people. Outside of How to Win Friends, this book has done more to help my professional and personal life than any other book I've read. It's also fun to read.
- ***Rich Dad, Poor Dad* by Robert Kiyosaki** - Another easy and usable book, this time about money. Kiyosaki is a born teacher with a passion for cutting through the confusion and myths about money and explaining the simple ways to a secure financial life.

Magazines
- ***Fast Company Magazine*** - The best coverage of business and leadership trends available. I also recommend it because they always cover what's going on in the arts too.
- ***Inc. Magazine*** - This is a business magazine focused on the people that run businesses and the issues they face everyday. I hope that explains why I recommend this magazine.

Online
- ***Seth Godin's Blog*** (http://sethgodin.typepad.com/ or,

http://sethgodin.com/) - If you read only one blog, make it this one. I don't know what to call Seth other than a genius at spotting trends and encouraging people to jump on them. In his own words, he: "riffs on marketing, respect, and the ways ideas spread." Check out his books, too.

Course
- **Dale Carnegie's Effective Communications & Human Relations** - As mentioned earlier in this chapter.

Last Thoughts

Thank you for taking the time to read *Why I Failed in the Creative Arts and How NOT to Follow in My Footsteps*. Congratulations on taking this important - and perhaps first - step toward your career.

I invite you to visit, bookmark and subscribe to whyifailed.com. In addition to my blog and links to where we can connect online, you'll find updated lists of resources you can use to NOT follow in my footsteps.

I hope to see you there.

For more ideas on how NOT to follow in Steve's footsteps, visit: www.whyifailed.com

www.ingramcontent.com/pod-product-compliance
Lightning Source LLC
Chambersburg PA
CBHW070731220326
41598CB00024BA/3386